by Jennifer Richard Jacobson

Reviewed by the
Parent-Teacher Advisory Board

Developmental Overview by Nancy Richard

becker & mayer!
BOOKS

SIMON & SCHUSTER

HOW IS MY FIRST GRADER DOING IN SCHOOL?

What to Expect and How to Help

Simon & Schuster
Rockefeller Center
1230 Avenue of the Americas
New York, NY 10020

becker & mayer!
BOOKS

Produced by becker&mayer!

Copyright © 1998 by Jennifer Richard Jacobson

DESIGNED BY BARBARA MARKS

Assessment booklet designed by Heidi Baughman
Interior illustrations by Cary Pillo and Dan Minnick
becker&mayer! art director: Simon Sung
becker&mayer! editor: Jennifer Worick

Manufactured in the United States of America

1 3 5 7 9 10 8 6 4 2

Library of Congress Cataloging-in-Publication Data
Jacobson, Jennifer, date.
     How is my first grader doing in school? : what to expect and how to
help / by Jennifer Richard Jacobson.
         p.   cm.
     1. First grade (Education)—United States.   2. Education,
Primary—Parent participation—United States.   3. Language arts
(Primary)—United States.   4. Mathematics—Study and teaching
(Primary)—United States.   I. Title.
LB1571.1stJ33   1998
372.24'1—dc21   98-15711
                                                                CIP

ISBN 0-684-84708-6

Acknowledgments

I would like to give special thanks to my mother and mentor, Nancy Richard, who wrote the Developmental Overview for this book. Wife, proud mother, and now doting grandmother, Nancy has been a student of child development, school readiness, and effective classroom practices for thirty years. As a consultant on the national lecture staff of the Gesell Institute of Human Development and a consulting teacher for the Northeast Foundation for Children, Nancy worked with thousands of teachers and parents throughout the country to promote classrooms that are educationally successful as well as responsive to the developmental needs of children. She coauthored *One Piece of the Puzzle: A School Readiness Manual.*

In addition, I would like to thank the members of our Parent Teacher Advisory Board who volunteered countless hours to reading and evaluating the books in this series. They have graciously shared their educational knowledge and insight. Their wisdom, gathered through years of working with children in classrooms, has enriched these books tremendously. Their guidance has been invaluable. Members of the Parent Teacher Advisory Board are as follows:

Jim Grant, a former teacher and principal, is an internationally known consultant and one of America's most passionate advocates for children. He is the founder of the Society for Developmental Education, the nation's primary provider of staff development training for elementary teachers. He is also founder and co–executive director of the National Alliance of Multiage Educators and the author of dozens of professional articles and educational materials. His books—*"I Hate School!" Some Common-Sense Answers for Educators and Parents Who Want to Know Why and What to Do About It, Retention and Its Prevention,* and *A Common-Sense Guide to Multiage Practices*—are recognized resources for teachers, parents, and administrators.

Mary Mercer Krogness, a public school teacher for over thirty years, is the recipient of the Martha Holden Jennings Master Teacher Award, the highest recognition the Martha Holden Jennings Foundation bestows on a classroom teacher in Cleveland, Ohio. She has taught grades k–8 in both urban and suburban schools and is currently a language arts consultant for five school systems, an educational speaker, and an author. In addition to award-winning articles, Mary is the author of *Just Teach Me, Mrs. K: Talking, Reading, and Writing with Resistant Adolescent Learners* and the writer-producer of an award-winning, nationally disseminated PBS television series, *Tyger, Tyger, Burning Bright,* a creative writing program for elementary age students.

Nancy O'Rourke, an early childhood specialist, has been a teacher for sixteen years. Most recently, she has taught in a first and second grade multiage classroom. Well recognized for her contributions to her Maine school system, Nancy has served on the early childhood task force, developed math and science curriculum, and helped create school-wide benchmarks for grades k-3 in math, science, and the humanities. Nancy also brings her role as a parent of two school-age children to her role as adviser.

Robert "Chip" Wood is a cofounder of the Northeast Foundation for Children, a nonprofit educational foundation whose mission is the improvement of education in elementary and middle schools. The foundation provides training, consultation, and professional development opportunities for teachers and administrators. It also operates a k-8 laboratory school for children and publishes articles and books written by teachers for educators and parents. Chip has served NEFC as a classroom teacher, consultant, and executive director. He is the author of many professional articles and the book *Yardsticks: Children in the Classroom, Ages 4–14,* and coauthor of *A Notebook for Teachers: Making Changes in the Elementary Curriculum.*

I would like to thank the talented staff at becker&mayer, who produced this book, especially Jim Becker, who offered this idea to me; Andy Mayer, who has followed it through; Jennifer Worick, who graciously navigated this book through all channels; Simon Sung, who coordinated the art; Heidi Baughman, who designed the assessment booklet; Jennifer Doyle, who worked with panel members; Dan Minnick, who drew computer sketches; and Kelly Skudlarick, who worked on the original proposal.

I would also like to acknowledge the members of the Simon & Schuster publishing group, particularly Trish Todd, who has shared our vision and commitment to this series; Cherise Grant, who has been engaged in all aspects of production; Barbara Marks, who designed the book; Toni Rachiele, who shepherded the book through production; and Marcela Landres, who did a little bit of everything.

I especially want to thank my coauthor on this series, Dottie Raymer. Although we have written separate pages, we have worked jointly every step of the way. Our philosophical discussions on education, teaching, and parenting have infused these books with our deepest convictions. It's been a wonderful collaboration.

And finally I would like to thank the countless teachers, parents, and children who have offered their knowledge, anecdotes, insights, artwork, and advice. I hope you recognize your contributions in these pages.

For Jake

Contents

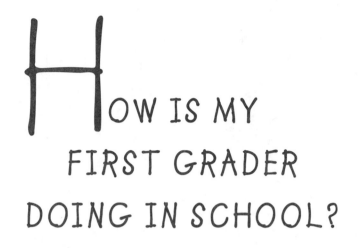

How is my
First Grader
doing in school?

Introduction

You were your child's first teacher. You are still your child's best teacher. No one knows your child better than you. No one knows how your child learns, his strengths and abilities, his interests, and what motivates him the way you do.

Research studies have shown time and time again that children whose parents are involved in their education are happier and more successful in school. Imagine this scenario. Several first graders are sitting on a rug, exploring small colored cubes. The teacher takes a handful of cubes and lays them carefully in a line: red, yellow, red, yellow. "That's a pattern!" shouts six-year-old José. "My father showed me how to make patterns." The teacher asks José if he would like to show the class another pattern. "Yes!" he says. He demonstrates the AABB pattern of red, red, yellow, yellow. Later that night, while his father reads him a story, José points out a pattern in one of the pictures of his book. "That's a tessellating pattern," his father says. "See how all of these shapes fit together without any spaces showing?" "Yes," says José. "Those shapes are triangles."

José is a confident learner. He experiences success, shares his knowledge, and is eager to learn more. His interactions are an example of the natural and spontaneous way that schooling and home education can go hand and hand.

Supporting your child's education does not necessarily mean devoting more time to teaching her. If your child is schooled away from home, she has a full day of learning and you have your job or other obligations. Instead, it means using the time you already have together in a different, more creative way. By discovering your child's strength's and weaknesses, you can capitalize on the time you have together. Every skill presented in this book can be reinforced in meaningful, brief exchanges like the one between José and his father.

Some parents show great determination in teaching their children. They buy workbooks and flash cards. They drill their children on math computation. But, in truth, a five-minute activity shared with you in the spirit of exploration, discovery, and affection can be far more beneficial for your child than thirty minutes of workbook completion. True learning occurs when a child is personally and actively involved in a project. It is also enhanced when accompanied by joy, curiosity, contentment, and persistence. When you take a few moments to investigate with your child, you are combining all the elements of an optimum learning situation.

Sometimes all it takes to support your child is lots of free time and the right nudge. One mother suggested that her children create a store on a rainy Saturday. With just that note of inspiration, the children decided that their store would be a pet shop. They gathered all their stuffed animals and made a chart to determine what each animal needed for proper food, space, and play. After they completed the chart and made the spaces, they gathered, packaged, and priced appropriate "food." Next, with the help of a computer, they wrote and printed an advertising flyer, giving complete descriptions of the pets. And finally the pet store was open for business, complete with adding machine to total prices and calculate change. While playing pet store, these children were learning and reinforcing skills in three areas: reading, writing, and math.

Knowing when and how to give your child a nudge is what this book is all about. It is intended to help you learn more about your child, more about what goes on in schools, and more about how to find the "teachable moment" so you can help your child reach his full potential.

Near the front of this book you will find an observational assessment. The observational assessment has three components: the For Kids Only booklet found in the envelope on the inside back cover, the Parent Observation Pages on page 34, and the Assessment Guide on page 53, and is divided into three parts: Math Assessment, Writing Assessment, and Reading Assessment. It is not a standardized test. It will not measure your child's IQ or creativity. Instead, it is meant to be a relaxed, informal way for you to find out where your child is on a learning continuum and what you can do to support him. Please read How to Use This Book, page 30, before beginning the assessment to ensure the very best results in gathering information.

The observational assessment will help you present to your child the ideas, skills, and concepts that are the most timely and appropriate. This is not to say that all learning moves in a straight line. It doesn't. But some skills are basic and need to be developed thoroughly before new concepts are introduced. It is not appropriate, for instance, to ask your child to add numbers before he is able to count, or to memorize spelling words before he has identified the sounds of the alphabet. The accompanying assessment will allow you to determine precisely which skills you would do best to focus on right now and which you should put off until a more suitable time.

The learning activities in *How Is My First Grader Doing in School?* cover the broad strokes of the first grade reading, writing, and math curriculum. This book is not meant to be all-inclusive. Your child will probably be exposed to concepts such as identifying nouns or basic fractions, which are not included in this book. At the first grade level these topics are introductory and usually given only brief exposure. This book is intended to reinforce the skills your child will be practicing regularly throughout the first grade.

Likewise, science, social studies, the arts, and physical education are not covered in this book. The content in these subject areas varies greatly from school to school and cannot be fairly presented here. Nevertheless, they are essential to a well-rounded education. In fact they promote and extend the learning your child does in the three R's. You may want to talk to your child's teacher or school specialists to learn how to support your child in these areas.

Developmental Overview

by Nancy Richard

What a momentous year this is! Your child is embarking on her school career. Although kindergarten was a milestone, the jumble of feelings you felt a year ago was probably only a glimmer of the emotions you experienced when your child entered what many consider "real school." The long academic day, the demand for children to learn reading, writing, and symbolic math; routines like lunches, buses, and bells create greater expectations for you and your child.

The First Grade Classroom

You may have a picture in your mind of what a first grade classroom will look like: children seated at rows of desks, lots of chalkboards, a flag, a clock, silhouettes of George Washington and Abraham Lincoln on the bulletin board. There will be a tall shelf of textbooks and, of course, up front in the middle a teacher's great big desk. You can even smell the crayons, the paste, the chalk, and hear the bells, the ticking clock, and the voices of children during recess.

Your own child's classroom, however, may look very different. A peek through the door might reveal children gathered around a table writing in journals; children curled up with stuffed animals and pillows, reading books in the library corner; and children working on a rug with math games. Bulletin boards are covered with children's artwork and writing, and there is a display shelf for things children have made or brought from home. There is an art area, a block area, and a place for computers.

One six-year-old is kneeling on her chair, her bottom up, with torso, arms, and book extended over the table. You notice that there is a lot of sprawling, movement, and activity in first grade. And there is quite a bit of noise. Two children painting at the easel are humming. One boy is loudly blowing air out of his mouth and tapping his head with his pencil as he tries to figure out a math problem. Another is slapping down his pencil on his clipboard as he finishes copying a design he has just completed with the pattern blocks.

At first glance, first grade may seem unorganized and a bit chaotic. Actually it is highly structured through careful arrangement of furniture and materials, and through careful planning of activities and work periods. One of the basic needs of first graders is a predictability in the environment: routines and rituals, a daily schedule they can count on, as well as friendly, fair, and consistent discipline.

Physical Development

As you've probably noticed, first graders are in constant motion. At home, they wiggle and fidget at the dinner table, flinging their arms out and knocking over their milk. They kneel on their chairs and drape themselves across the table to write or color. They sprawl on the floor to watch TV. At school they have to be allowed to move their bodies or tension will cause them to wiggle from side to side on their chairs and fall out, or even to tip the chair over backwards. Even when the children are being allowed movement, chairs always seem to be falling over. Many first graders work best while sprawled out on the floor or standing up. Outside, they run around, chase each other, and challenge gravity on the climbing apparatus. The muscle growth at this age, and the need to exercise, turns the sixth to seventh year into an age of gusto.

In a developmental stage of marked imbalance, first graders bump into and fall over each other at recess like a string of dominoes. They seem not to see the playground apparatus, balls, other children, or adults. When confronted with this, first graders will looked perplexed and say, "I didn't see it" or "I didn't see you."

First grade children appear to be strong auditory processors. They learn by listening to others and to themselves. They often repeat everything out loud so they can understand it. This is one of the reasons that first grade classes seem so noisy: the talking out of instructions, thoughts, even ideas. "Oh, I get it!" is often heard as they show their sudden insight. Those children who can read with some fluency will subvocalize, or whisper, the words. Because of this auditory preference, first grade is a good time to teach phonics (sounds of letters).

If you keep hearing "What?" when you speak to your child, it may not be that your child doesn't hear you. Everyone has a way to buy time when thinking out a problem or answering a question. First graders buy this time by repeating what you ask or by asking you to repeat it.

In many first graders, the use of small muscles, or fine motor control, has not yet matured. So writing , especially formal writing, can be agony for them. Usually by spring, those muscles are under a lot more command, and you'll see a greatly improved product.

The way children hold their pencils is also related to physical development and not a learned procedure. Teachers have tried for years to correct this so that children have the appropriate grip. Today, it's questionable whether this is possible or even desirable. If your first grader is holding her pencil with the middle finger and thumb rather than the index finger and thumb, this is probably just a young grip. It is the one most commonly seen in kindergarten. By first grade, most children will be using what we think of as the proper grip, the pencil grasped by the thumb and index finger, with the middle finger underneath for control. A very unusual grip probably indicates that your child best controls the pencil that way. If her writing or drawing is legible, leave her pencil grip alone. If she is frustrated with the outcome, you might buy or ask her teacher about a plastic device called a pencil grip to help your child grasp it better. You might also buy some special three-sided pencils shaped like a pencil grip.

Writing on lines is very difficult for some first graders, and their writing tends to be inconsistent, large, and sloppy. Their brains are working hard on remembering what letter to use, and how to make it, sometimes even what sound it makes, so quality is not a priority. Giving your child a choice of lined or unlined paper may help. In fact, the more choices she has in the kind of paper and writing utensils available for use, the higher her likelihood for success. This is true for every child.

The formation of letters is often difficult for first graders. Parents usually teach children their names in capital letters (uppercase letters). Their intuition is correct here. The capital letters are easier for children to write and to recognize. They can still read the small letters (lowercase) even if they are writing in capitals. Teachers who are not confined to a

My family.

rigid curriculum often let children interchange the uppercase and lowercase letters in their writing. When this is allowed, the first lower case letter that children spontaneously use is the *i* (see art on opposite page). They love making a line and a big fat dot. The last lowercase letters they'll use are *b*, *d*, *q*, and *k*. Interestingly, these are the letters they have the most difficulty with, and those most often reversed.

Another thing that is difficult visually for most first graders is copying from the chalkboard. If your child is having trouble with this, ask her teacher if there is another way for her to do the work. Often children who have difficulty copying from the blackboard *can* copy from something beside them. It's the shift from near to far vision that is difficult. They love to work at the blackboard themselves.

Children are constantly showing us how they need to learn. Like plants leaning toward light and pushing their roots toward water, children gravitate toward those things that appropriately support them in doing their best work.

Emotional Development

Emotionally, first graders are known for their giddiness. They now see the humor in the Amelia Bedelia stories. They're ripe for the whimsy of *Winnie the Pooh*. Often called the six-year-old sillies, they enjoy jokes, riddles, and risqué language. In fact, the use of bathroom words returns. They can go into gales of laughter over such words as "but," "bottom," and "underwear." Teachers often capitalize on this love of the absurd as they plan their teaching strategies.

For instance, while observing your child's class you might see the teacher reading the big book *Mrs. Wishy-Washy*, a story about animals getting a bath. Giggling erupts as they see the pig, butt up, in the tub. "What sounds do you hear in the words 'wishy' and 'washy'?" asks the teacher. *"Sh-sh-sh"* chime the children. "Who knows another word that has that sound?" All hands go up. "She" says one child. "Shoe," adds another. A third, with a glimmer in her eye snickers, "Fishy-gishy." If you share a special joke with your first grader, she will share it with her friends and teacher over and over again.

First graders can leave home with ease. At school, they go to the water cooler and to other areas of the school on their own. They like planning a project with one or two other children, or putting on a play. This seeming independence, a hallmark of first graders, is refreshing for parents and teachers after the tendency to cling and the need to check in that was so prevalent in kindergarten. It is *seeming* independence, however, because first graders are still very dependent on their parents and teacher for support and approval. And as they venture out, they need to know that things are intact at home.

First grade is often called the superlative year. Your first grader wants to be the biggest, the best, the one you love the most. She is boisterous and enthusiastic, and she loves adventure. She likes anything new: games, ideas, places. She loves learning and showing off her many new accomplishments. It's important that you notice how fast she can run and that you see that she used some fancy words in her writing this morning. This kind of encouragement is the fuel she runs on. She can also be a braggart. If you don't admire the things she does, she'll admire them herself. (It may interest you to know that at school she brags about you.)

As much as she likes newness and beginning almost anything, your first grader tires very easily and gets frequent illnesses. She can't stick to activities for very long. Even on the best of days, she often comes home from school very fatigued, and she takes this fatigue out on you. It may take the form of tantrums, refusal to take direction, or crying. She can be disrespectful verbally and physically, especially if she detects the slightest bit of criticism. She probably doesn't want to be drilled about what she did at school today, nor does she care to tell you what's wrong. The chances are, she doesn't know! She's just exhausted. As she reaches age six and a half to seven, this tendency should even out.

The more rituals and routines you can establish, the more your child will feel safe and cared for. First graders need the comfort of predictability when they themselves are changing so rapidly. So a morning routine with an affectionate good-bye and a bedtime routine with a story and a special hug are important. Make sure your child knows exactly what will happen after school: who will be at home or who will pick her up for day care. Any uncertainty about home can keep her distracted all day at school.

A trait you've probably seen in your first grader, and one that is hard to deal with, is her difficulty with decision-making. She can't seem to decide what to eat, what to wear, what to do. This can cause her and everyone around her a great deal of emotional turmoil. School mornings can be more pleasant and productive if her choices are limited.

Try setting out two complete outfits for her the night before. When she gets up, let her decide between the two. Characteristically, she'll decide on one, and then choose the second. For breakfast, a simple "Do you want puffed wheat or corn flakes?" is enough of a choice. Or you may want her to make out a breakfast chart and a wardrobe chart as part of Saturday's routine. Whatever you do, don't get into a power struggle over choices. It's just not worth it. Your first grader can be very oppositional and stubborn.

Sixes hate to lose, and they cannot take criticism. So it's important to choose activities that they can succeed at, or at least where the potential for success is highly likely. If things get too competitive, they will change the rules so that they can win, or they'll refuse to play anymore. One young man is known to have asked his grandfather, "Does this game have a winner?" The more accurate question would have been, "Does this game have a loser?"

Occasionally it works the other way around, but usually your first grader is an angel at school and a devil at home. The kind of parent who is most helpful to the sometimes fresh, sometimes friendly, but always feisty first grader is a *cheerleader*. Cheer her on through her industrious but awkward attempts at reading and writing. Cheer her on as she navigates the rough waters of adjusting to a more demanding environment and sometimes stormy relationships. Ignore her quarrelsomeness and fretting as much as possible. Carefully examine the stories she brings home from school, or at least check them out before you act on them. They will often be exaggerated, and some of them will be completely untrue. By tomorrow she will usually have forgotten them. Six- to seven-year-olds are also very much concerned with justice—in other words, they tattle. Sometimes this tattling is a way for children to make sure that *you* know that *they* know the rules. The wise parent will listen and commiserate but not take sides.

Maintaining a good relationship with your first grader's teacher during the year, and checking in periodically, will be welcomed by your child's teacher. When the two of you have shared goals for your child, you can support each other in many ways. Volunteer some of your time to the classroom if you can. At least find time to visit. It's especially important that you see your child in relationship to her peers.

This is one of the most important years in your child's school life. The underpinnings for the rest of her school career are being established. The activities that follow have been carefully planned to be fun and challenging and to support what she'll be learning in first grade. Bon voyage!

Questions and Answers About First Grade

What is "normal" for first grade?

Perhaps most startling is the wide range of abilities and achievement levels of the children. Some first graders are just learning to say letter sounds, while others are reading chapter books. Some children are labeling pictures with a few letters, while others are writing long stories that include punctuation. Some children are learning to count, while others are exploring metric measurement on the computer. This range is normal and expected in the first grade classroom. To most parents' relief, all of these children are considered on target. With assistance and special planning on the teacher's part, children can work on the same content in a way that meets each child's specific needs.

My first grader has not begun to read yet. Should I be concerned?

Not all first graders are ready to read. In fact, some children don't read fluently until age seven or eight. It's important to remember that your child's developmental level (the functioning of his muscles, eyes, ears, and nervous system) is operating on its own timetable. In most first grades the developmental range varies widely, and therefore the readiness for reading also varies.

Visually, those first graders who are ready to read are beginning to see detail. If you draw a symbol, such as a circle with half of it shaded in, and ask them what it is, they'll give you detail—"A circle, half colored, half not"—instead of a single-word response like "ball" or "circle." Their eyes can now move across a line of print with relative ease, although some may have trouble consistently moving from left to right.

What is the best method of teaching children to read?

A good deal of controversy surrounds the best way to teach children to read. In recent years the warring factions appear to be those that are proponents of an integrated, or whole language, approach (teaching children to focus on meaning and skills while reading good literature) and supporters of phonics methods (teaching children to decode words in a structured, sequenced manner).

It's surprising that this debate has continued as long as it has. In many ways asking which is better, whole language or phonics, is like asking which is the better way to eat, by chewing or by swallowing? The answer, of course, is that the best way to eat is to chew *and* swallow.

The same is true of reading. Skilled readers do not use a single strategy, but a combination of strategies. A beginning reader who uses context only to determine what a word means is likely to guess too often. He or she may not be able to move beyond books that are highly repetitive or those that provide strong picture clues. A beginning reader who uses phonics only to determine what a word means is apt to become frustrated, lack fluency, or recite words without understanding what is being read.

In the best of classrooms, teachers use a variety of literature and ask children to predict the meaning of words based on what they know, what would make sense, and what sounds the words incorporate. In other words, they use the best of all methods.

My child is being encouraged to use invented spelling. Why should he learn this system when he is going to have to learn to spell correctly eventually?

When your child was learning to talk, she probably said words like "da" for Daddy and "ba-ba" for bottle. You enjoyed these early talking efforts because you knew that the words would eventually evolve into standard speech. Invented spelling, or better yet, practice spelling, as many schools now call it, is similar to early speech. It is your child's first attempts at communicating through writing.

Practice spelling is not a chancy way to learn. Children pass through distinct and predictable stages on their way to learning to spell conventionally. Here is the most common sequence children go through using the word "spell" as an example.

s   Initially, children write just the beginning sound for each word.
sl   Next, they write the first and last sounds of words.
spl   The child begins to hear and write the sounds of median consonants.

spal   Children become aware of vowels in words. They often use one
        vowel, frequently the letter *a*, as a marker for all vowels.

spell   The writer now differentiates between different vowel sounds and
        has seen the word often enough to remember that there are two *l*'s at
        the end of it.

The joy of practice spelling is that it allows children to write creatively without the inappropriate pressure to write perfectly. At the end of first grade or the beginning of second grade, children are ready for a more formal spelling program. By this time they have grown as confident, expressive writers.

(For more information about the stages of writing development see pages 104–16.)

My child reverses some letters and numbers. Is this a sign that she may be dyslexic?

Not at all. It is normal for first graders to write numbers and letters backwards. The children know they're reversing them. They say such things as "I can write them, but I make them backwards," or "Sometimes it comes out right and sometimes it comes wrong, and I can't tell what way is right and what way is wrong." These reversals are transitory. They usually disappear when children are seven or seven and a half.

It's better not to make too big an issue of these reversals. Instead, say to your child, "Children sometimes write backwards. When you get older, you won't do it anymore." It's like training wheels on a bicycle. The children know they're not permanent and that one day they'll be able to ride without them.

Why isn't my first grader bringing home math papers?

Math is not simply computation; it's an understanding of number and spatial relationships. Children come by this deeper understanding by working with real things: connecting cubes, pattern blocks, beans, and place-value boards. By manipulating these objects, your child will come to truly know what numbers are—symbols for real things—and how they work.

There is no need to rush the first grader into doing symbolic paper-and-pencil tasks. Once your child has spent many hours exploring, counting, measuring, adding, and subtracting concrete objects, he'll have little difficulty recording his knowledge on paper.

My child still counts on her fingers. How can I get her to stop?

As mentioned above, children learn about math from experience with concrete objects. What objects are easier to use and more readily available than fingers?

As children learn to add and subtract and to memorize math facts—a skill that comes with much practice in working with real things—they will no longer need to compute on their fingers, at least not all the time (Fess up. Did you use fingers when figuring your taxes?). Think of this practice as a bridge to learning, not an obstacle.

Should my first grader have homework?

Only if the homework is appropriate. Some schools ask that a first grader read for six minutes each night (this time increases with the child's age) or that a parent and child read together twice a week from a special book bag. Having your child read for a brief time or reading to your child is always appropriate.

On the other hand, regular homework assignments for the first grader may not be beneficial. As mentioned, first graders come home from school exhausted. They have already given every ounce of energy to schoolwork and need to do other things at home such as playing hopscotch or fighting dragons from the front stoop.

If your school insists on giving homework to first graders, request that the homework be open-ended, creative projects instead of busywork such as fill-in-the-answer worksheets. For instance, one teacher of first and second graders had her children design a nest for a bird while trying to meet certain criteria: the nest had to be warm, and it had to be large enough and strong enough to support a hen's egg. The results of the homework assignment were astonishing. Children made nests from hollowed-out pumpkins, discarded food containers, yarn, pot holder loops, homemade Play-Doh, and natural materials such as sticks and grass. Homework assignments like this are advantageous because they help children apply what they know in new and creative ways.

How to Use This Book

A. Participate in the observational assessment.

Assessment is a natural process for parents. Every time you asked your young child a question such as *"Can you say 'Dada'?"* or *"Where is your nose?"* or *"What color is this?"* you were collecting information and using that information to determine what to teach your child next. If you had questions, you found a list of the developmental stages of learning. By observing your child and asking the right questions, you were able to support your child's learning.

You may have found, however, that ever since your child reached school age, it has been a greater challenge to maintain the role of supportive coach. It's hard to get a clear understanding of what is expected of your child. Without specific knowledge of the curriculum, you may not know the questions to ask. The purpose of this book and the accompanying assessment is to help you continue to observe your child with awareness.

The word "assessment" comes from roots that mean "to sit beside." The informal assessment is a way for you to sit beside your child and collect the information you need. Once you have observed your child, you will be guided to activities that encourage you and your child to continue to learn together.

Remember, the assessment is not a standardized test. It will not tell you how your child compares to other children in the nation. It will not even tell you how your child compares with your neighbors' children. But it will give you a starting point for determining how to increase your child's confidence and success in learning.

Here are the steps you will follow:

1. **Take the "For Kids Only" booklet out of the envelope in the back of the book and read through it one time.** This will familiarize you with the visuals that you will be presenting to your child. Cut out the ruler and shapes on the back cover of the booklet.

2. **Photocopy and read the Parent Observation Pages (page 34).** Reading these pages ahead of time will help you to see how the child booklet and your instructions are coordinated. It will also allow you to decide how much of the assessment you want to give to your child at one sitting. Even if you think your child will be able to respond to most of these questions, it is recommended that you give the three parts of the assessment (math, writing, and reading) at different times. You may even decide to divide the three parts into even smaller sections to suit your child's attention span or your particular time schedule.

3. **Provide a place to give the assessment that is relatively free of distractions.** Talk to your first grader about the activities. Tell your child that you want to learn more about him and that these activities will teach *you*. Make sure you approach the activity in a lighthearted manner.

4. **Above all, keep the assessment fun and relaxed for your child.** If your child is afraid to try an activity, don't push him. After all, that is valuable information for you, too. Whenever your child has difficulty with a reading passage or math problem, *stop* and skip ahead to the question your Parent Observation Pages recommend. There is never a reason to work above your child's comfort level.

5. **Give positive reinforcement as often as possible.** You might say, "I didn't know you could do that!" or "When did you get so smart?" If your child seems upset or confused by an exercise, let him off the hook. You might say, "That question is confusing, isn't it?" Make sure your child ends the assessment feeling successful. One way of doing this is to return to a question your child can answer with obvious ease. Say, "I forgot to write your answer down. Can you show me how you did this problem again?"

B. Use the Assessment Guide, page 53, to find out what your child knows and what he is ready to learn next.

If you find that a question on the assessment did not give you enough information, or if you are confused about your child's response, you may want to talk to his teacher. See the last chapter, "Working With Your Child's Teacher," for more information.

C. Turn to the appropriate activity pages to learn more about how and why specific skills are taught and how you can help your first grader acquire these skills.

In each skill area, activities are suggested under two headings: "Have Five Minutes?" and "Have more time?" Some of the activities in the five-minute section are quick games that you and your child can play while waiting for dinner, riding in the car, or walking to the bus stop. Others are activities that you can explain within five minutes and then let your child complete on his own. Activities in the "Have more time?" category require more planning or a longer time commitment on your part.

Do not feel that you should do every activity listed under a skill heading. A number of different activities are provided so you can choose the ones that appeal to you and your child. And don't feel guilty if you haven't tried something new for a while. If you do only a couple of these exercises occasionally, you will give your first grader a genuine boost toward success. You'll be amazed at how a question here and a three-minute activity there can demonstrate to your child how much you value his ideas and his education. Feel free to adapt these activities to your needs.

You may want to go back and repeat some of the activities presented earlier in the book. Reviewing can yield wonderful benefits. When your child revisits a skill, he usually gains a deeper understanding—an understanding that he can apply to new learning. There are sure to be games in every area that your child will have great fun playing.

Should you pursue activities that seem more difficult for your child? Probably not. Pushing your child too fast may backfire. Rather than looking forward to the games you initiate, your child may associate them with confusion, boredom, or failure. It's good to remember that success is the greatest motivator of all.

Some of the activities are competitive. Many first grade children do not like competitive games and cannot handle them gracefully. If your child is noncompetitive, don't play against each other. Make yourselves a team instead, and try to beat the clock or another imaginary player (who always makes the most foolish decisions).

Repeat the assessment when appropriate.

After some time has gone by, perhaps a month or two, and you and your child have participated in many of the activities, you may want to repeat the assessment or a portion of it. By reassessing, you can determine if your child has grown in his understanding of concepts. The Assessment Guide will direct you to new areas of learning to focus on next.

If you choose not to give the entire assessment, make sure you ask some questions that you know your child will answer competently. *Always end the assessment on a positive note.*

Remember, the assessment is meant to be an informal tool for gathering information. You may want to adapt the questions or ask new questions to see if you first grader has truly mastered a skill.

Many teachers now assess children in the classroom by doing what one educator, Yetta Goodman, termed "kid watching." Kid watching is what parents have always done best. Have a ball watching your child grasp new knowledge.

Parent Observation Pages

Photocopy the Parent Observation Pages. Taking the time to photocopy the pages will allow you to match your child's responses to the answer guide more easily. It will also allow you to repeat the assessment with your child or to give the assessment to a sibling.

Ask your child the questions that appear in italics throughout the assessment, but do not feel that you must rigidly adhere to the wording. These questions are meant to be a guide, not a script. You may find other ways of questioning that are more suited to your own and your child's needs. For more information, see the preceding chapter, "How to Use this Book."

Math Assessment

Before beginning the math assessment, cut out the shapes and the ruler on the back cover of the assessment booklet. Have paper and pencil available for your child to use.

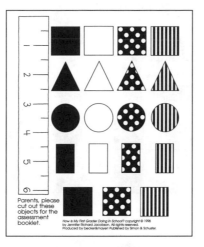

Use assessment booklet pages 2–3 for questions 1 and 2.

1. **Use pages 2–3 of the booklet.** *Can you tell me the name of these shapes?*
   Check all that apply.
   ___ Can name the square.
   ___ Can name the circle.
   ___ Can name the triangle.
   ___ Can name the rectangle.

2. Give your child the cutout shapes.
   How can you sort these?
   Can you find another way to sort these?
   Check one.
   ___ Can find **one way** to sort the shapes—for example, by shape or
   design.
   ___ Can find **two ways** to sort the shapes.
   ___ Cannot sort the shapes at this time.

*Use assessment
booklet pages 4–5
for questions
3 and 4.*

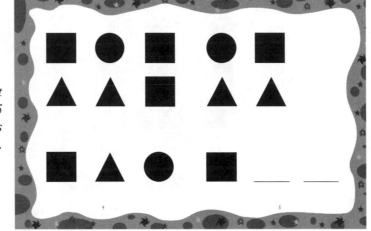

3. **Use pages 4–5.** Point to the first row. *Look at this row. Can you tell which
   shape will come next?*
   Point to the second row. *Now look at this row. Which shape will come next?*
   Check all that apply.
   ___ Can determine the shape for the first row (circle).
   ___ Can determine the shape for the second row (square).
   ___ Cannot determine the patterns at this time.

4. **Use pages 4–5.** Give your child the cutouts. Point to the third row. *Using
   these shapes, can you continue the pattern?*
   Check one.
   ___ Can extend the pattern (both shapes correct).
   ___ Cannot extend the pattern at this time.

5. *Using these shapes, can you make your own pattern?*
   Now can you make a different pattern?
   Check one.
   ___ Makes one pattern only.
   ___ Attempts two designs, but the patterns are the same. For instance,
   solid–polka dot–solid–polka dot and triangle-square-triangle-square
   would be the same **ABAB** pattern.
   ___ Creates two designs with two different patterns.
   ___ Cannot make a pattern at this time.

6. Place 5 cutout squares on the floor or the table, like this: □□□□□.
   How many squares are there?
   Check one.
   ___ Points to count correctly.
   ___ Counts correctly without pointing.
   ___ Does not count correctly at this time.

7. Now spread the same 5 squares out like this: □   □   □   □   □
   Now how many squares are there?
   Check one.
   ___ Points to count squares.
   ___ Does not point, but counts the squares again.
   ___ Automatically says "Five."
   ___ Does not count correctly at this time.

> If your child could not count the squares correctly in questions 6 and 7, *STOP*
> the Math Assessment here. Go on to the Writing Assessment, page 46.

8. Now add two more squares. *How many squares are there now?*
   Check one.
   ___ Uses finger to count squares.
   ___ Does not use finger but counts the squares again.
   ___ Automatically says "Seven."
   ___ Does not count correctly.

9. Point to the seven squares. *There are seven squares.*
   Cover up three squares with your hand. *How many squares are hiding?*
   Check one.
   ___ Correctly names number of squares hidden (3).
   ___ Cannot solve this problem at this time.

10. Place all seven squares together in a row. Cover six with your hand. *How many squares am I hiding now?*
    Check one.
    ___ Correctly names number of squares hidden (6).
    ___ Cannot solve this problem at this time.

Use assessment booklet pages 6–7 for questions 11 and 12.

11. **Use pages 6–7.** *Can you tell me the names of these numbers?*
    Circle the numbers your child cannot name at this time.

2	4	5	3	8
1	7	10	6	9

12. **Use pages 6–7.** *Can you point to the numbers from 1 to 10 in the correct order?*
    Check one.
    ___ Points to the numbers in the correct order.
    ___ Makes one or more mistakes but corrects himself.
    ___ Cannot point to the numbers in order at this time.

13. *How high can you count?*
    Check one.
    ___ Counts to 10 correctly.
    ___ Counts to 20 correctly.
    ___ Counts to 50 correctly.
    ___ Counts to 100 with one or two errors.
    ___ Counts to 100 with no errors.

> **I**f your child cannot count beyond 50, *STOP.* Skip ahead to question 18. If your child can count to 50, go on to question 14.

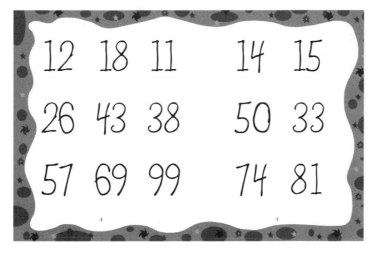

Use assessment booklet pages 8–9 for questions 14 and 15.

14. **Use pages 8–9.** *Tell me the names of these numbers.*
    Point to the numbers. Circle any **incorrect** responses.

12	18	11	14	15
26	43	38	50	33
57	69	99	74	81

15. **Use pages 8–9.** *What is the largest number in this row?*
    Point to each row and have your child identify the largest number.
    Check all that apply.
    ___ Points to 18 in the first row.
    ___ Points to 50 in the second row.
    ___ Points to 99 in the third row.
    ___ Cannot point correctly to any of the numbers at this time.

16. Draw 14 random dots on paper. Write the
    number 14. Then ask:
    *What does the 4 mean in this number? Can you
    circle that many counters?*
    *What does the 1 mean in this number? Can you
    circle that many counters?*

17. Can you count by
    Tens?   Yes, to ____.   Not at this time. ___
    Fives?   Yes, to ____.   Not at this time. ___
    Twos?   Yes, to ____.   Not at this time. ___

*Use assessment
booklet pages
10–11 for
questions 18
and 19.*

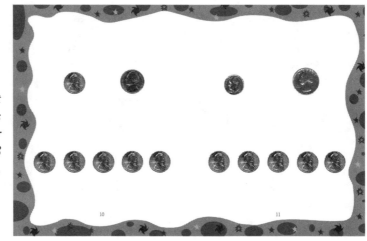

18. *Can you tell me the names of these coins?*
    Check all that apply.
    ___ Names a penny.
    ___ Names a nickel.
    ___ Names a dime.
    ___ Names a quarter.

19. **Use pages 10–11.** *Can you count these pennies?*
    Check one.
    ___ Counts the pennies accurately (10).
    ___ Makes a mistake but corrects herself.
    ___ Cannot count the pennies at this time.

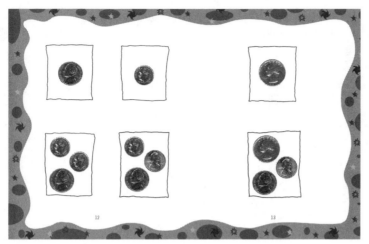

Use assessment booklet pages 12–13 for question 20.

20. **Use pages 12–13.** *How many cents are in each box?*
    Circle **incorrect** responses.

5¢	10¢	25¢
25¢	16¢	31¢

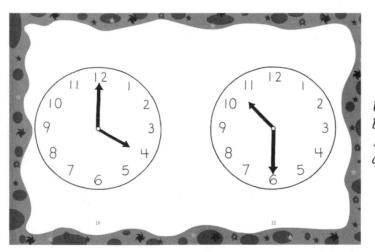

Use assessment booklet pages 14–15 for question 21.

21. **Use pages 14–15.** Point to the first clock.
    What time does this clock show?
    ___ 4:00   ___ Cannot tell at this time.
    If your child answered correctly, point to the second clock.
    What time does this clock show?
    ___ 10:30   ___ Cannot tell at this time.

*Use assessment
booklet pages
16–17 for
questions
22 and 23.*

22. **Use pages 16–17.** Give your child the cutout squares and ask, *Can you tell me how many squares long this pencil is?*
Check one.
___ Yes (6 squares)
___ Not at this time.

23. **Use pages 16–17.** Give your child the cutout ruler. *Can you tell me how long the crayon is in inches?*
___ Yes (3 inches)
___ Not at this time.

24. Hold out your index finger. *Can you guess how many squares long my finger is?*
Have your child guess, then use the cutout squares to check the guess.
___ Guesses between 2 and 6 squares (reasonable estimate).
___ Guesses less than 2 or more than 6 squares.

25. Place 15 cutout shapes in your hand. *How many shapes do you think I have in my hand?*
Have your child guess, then count the cutouts to check.
___ Guesses between 10 and 30 shapes (reasonable guess).
___ Guesses less than 9 or more than 30 shapes.

*Use assessment
booklet pages
18–19 for
question 26.*

26. **Use pages 18–19.** *I'm going to ask you some questions. Point to the number that makes the most sense.*
Check **correct** answers.
___ *Which number shows* about *how many raisins you could hold in your hand?* (20)
___ *Which number shows* about *how many cookies a person eats at one time?* (3)
___ *Which number shows* about *the number of pieces of cereal in your bowl at breakfast?* (86)

27. Read these word problems aloud to your child as many times as requested. Allow your child to use fingers, pencil and paper, or objects such as the cutouts to solve the problems.
A. *There are 9 turtles at the pet store. A woman decides to buy 4. How many turtles are left?* (5)
B. *Tom invites 5 friends to his birthday party. Then he changes his mind and invites 3 more. How many friends has he invited now?* (8)
Check all that apply.
___ Answers problem A correctly.
___ Answers problem B correctly.
___ Cannot answer either question correctly at this time.

28. What strategy did your child use to solve these problems? Check all that apply.
___ Used counters or other objects, including fingers.
___ Drew a picture.
___ Acted it out.
___ Made a list.
___ Used logical reasoning.

> **I**f your child answers one or both of these questions incorrectly, *STOP*. Skip ahead to question 31. If your child answered both questions correctly, go on to question 29.

29. If your child could correctly solve the two word problems above, read the following word problem aloud.
C. *There are 4 mice in the room. How many mouse ears are there? How many mice legs? (8, 16)*
Check all that apply.
___ Solved the first problem correctly.
___ Solved the second problem correctly.
___ Cannot solve these problems at this time.

30. What strategy did your child use to solve these problems? Check all that apply.
___ Used counters or other objects, including fingers.
___ Drew a picture.
___ Acted it out.
___ Made a list.
___ Used logical reasoning.

31. Copy the following addition problems on a sheet of paper. *Can you solve these problems?*

a. $4 + 5 =$	b. 6 $+ 3$	c. 7 $+ 8$	d. 9 $+ 4$	e. 13 $+ 72$	f. 26 $+ 41$

Circle the problems your child answered incorrectly.
a. (9) b. (9) c. (15) d. (13) e. (85) f. (67)

32. What strategies did your child use? If you don't know, point to individual problems and ask, *How did you solve this problem?*
Check all that apply.

___ Used objects, such as fingers.
___ Drew a picture.
___ Knew the answer (has memorized 4+5=9).
___ Counted on or up from the first number.
___ Made a double: "I knew that 7+7=14, so I added one."
___ Made a ten: "I added one to nine and then took one from four."
___ Added the right column, then the left column (in problems *e* and *f*).
___ Took the larger number and added tens first and then ones (*e* and *f*).
___ Other _____.

33. Copy the subtraction problems on paper. *Can you solve these problems?*

a. $9 - 4 =$	b. 7 $- 5$ ___	c. 16 $- 8$ ___	d. 14 $- 9$ ___	e. 56 $- 31$ ___	f. 68 $- 23$ ___

Circle problems answered **incorrectly.**

a. (5)   b. (2)   c. (8)   d. (5)   e. (25)   f. (45)

34. What strategies did your child use? If you don't know, point to individual problems and ask, *How did you solve this problem?*
Check all that apply.

___ Used objects, such as fingers.
___ Drew a picture.
___ Counted backwards.
___ Knew the answer (memorized 9 – 4 = 5).
___ Knew related facts (4 + 5 = 9 so 9 – 4 must equal 5).
___ Subtracted the right column, then the left column (with problems *e* and *f*).
___ Took the larger number and subtracted tens first and then ones. (*e* and *f*).
___ Other _____.

Writing Assessment

Have your child make a picture using the cutout shapes. Encourage your first grader to make any picture he or she wishes. When your child has completed the picture, provide him or her with a blank sheet of paper. Ask your child to write a story about the picture. This will provide you with a writing sample.

If your child does not want to make a shape picture, ask him or her to draw a picture. Then say, *Write some words about your picture.* If this isn't successful, ask your child's teacher for a current writing sample.

Reading Assessment

Use assessment booklet pages 20–21 for question 1.

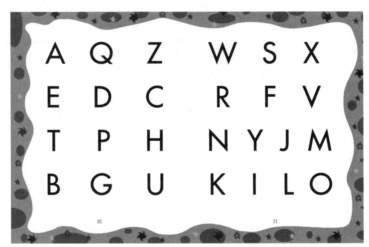

1. **Use pages 20–21.** *Can you tell me the names of these letters?*
   Circle the letters your child has difficulty naming.

A	Q	Z	W	S	X
E	D	C	R	F	V
T	P	H	N	Y	J	M
B	G	U	K	I	L	O

   ___ None

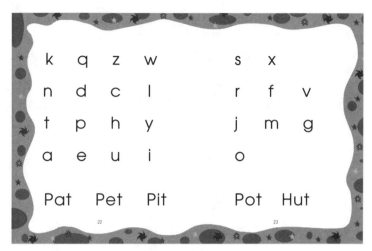

Use assessment booklet pages 22–23 for questions 2–4.

2. **Use pages 22–23.** *Can you tell me the names of these letters?*
   Circle the letters your child has difficulty naming.

   k   q   z   w   s   x
   n   d   c   l   r   f   v
   t   p   h   y   j   m   g
   a   e   u   i   o
   ___ None

3. **Use pages 22–23.** Point to each letter in the first three rows (skip the last
   row). *Can you tell me the sound this letter makes?* Some letters, such as *c*
   and *g*, have more than one sound. Accept any correct response.
   Circle the letters your child had difficulty identifying by their sound.

   k   q   z   w   s   x
   n   d   c   l   r   f   v
   t   p   h   y   j   m   g
   ___ None

4. **Use pages 22–23.** *Can you read these words?*
   Circle the words your child **can** read.

   pat   pet   pit   pot   hut

Use assessment booklet pages 24–25 for questions 5 and 6.

5. **Use pages 24–25.** *Can you read this story?* Encourage your child to look at the pictures and make a prediction. If your child can't get started, read the first box aloud.
   Check one.
   ___ Does not attempt to read the story.
   ___ Attempts to read the story after I read the first box, but has difficulty.
   ___ Determines most or all of the words after I read the first box.
   ___ Reads most or all of the words independently.

6. **Use pages 24–25.** Point to the box without any words and ask: *If there were words on this page, what do you think they would say?*
   Check one.
   ___ Does not offer a suggestion.
   ___ Provides a response that matches the story pattern (we hug, we kiss, we say good-bye).
   ___ Provides a response, but it does not match the story pattern.

If your child did not attempt to read this story, or could not "read" this story, *STOP* the Reading Assessment here.

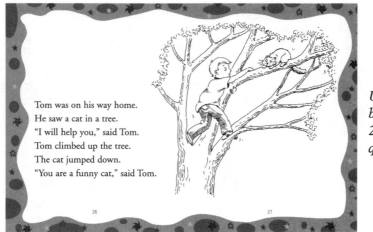

Use assessment booklet pages 26–27 for questions 7–9.

7. **Use pages 26–27.** *Can you read this story?* If you child stops at a word, give him or her a moment to figure it out. If necessary, supply the word and encourage your child to continue.
   Circle the words your child has difficulty reading.

   > Tom was on his way home.
   > He saw a cat in a tree.
   > "I will help you," said Tom.
   > Tom climbed up the tree.
   > The cat jumped down.
   > "You are a funny cat," said Tom.

   ___ None

8. What does your child do to figure out a word he or she doesn't know? Check all that apply:
   ___ Looks at pictures.
   ___ Guesses based on context.
   ___ Sounds it out.
   ___ Knew all the words.

9. **Use pages 26–27.** Can your child answer these questions? Check all **correct** answers.
   ___ A. *Where was Tom going?* (home)
   ___ B. *What did he see?* (a cat in a tree)
   ___ C. *What happened next?* (Tom tried to help the cat, but the cat jumped down.)

___ D. *Why do you think Tom called the cat funny?* (Check if your child gave a response to the question.)

___ E. *What would you do if you were Tom?* (Check if your child gave a response to the question.)

If your child stopped at 5 or more words in the previous story, STOP the Reading Assessment here.

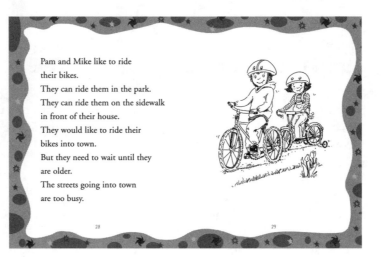

Use assessment booklet pages 28–29 for questions 10–12.

10. **Use pages 28–29.** If your child stopped at fewer than 5 words in the above story, ask, *Can you read this story?* If your child stops at a word, give him or her a moment to figure it out. If necessary, supply the word and encourage your child to continue.

    Circle the words your child has difficulty reading.

    Pam and Mike like to ride their bikes.
    They can ride them in the park.
    They can ride them on the sidewalk in front of their house.
    They would like to ride their bikes into town.
    But they need to wait until they are older.
    The streets going into town are too busy.

    ___ None

11. What does your child do to figure out a word he or she doesn't know? Check all that apply.

    ___ Looks at pictures.

___ Guesses based on context.
___ Sounds it out.
___ Knew all the words.

12. **Use pages 28–29.** Can your child answer these questions? Check all **correct** answers.
    ___ A. *What do Pam and Mike like to do?* (ride their bikes)
    ___ B. *Where can Pam and Mike ride their bikes?* (to the park, on the sidewalk)
    ___ C. *What does the word "busy" mean in this story?* (the roads have heavy traffic)
    ___ D. In what ways are you like Pam and Mike? In what ways are you different from them? (Check if your child gave a response to the question.)

I f your child stopped at 5 or more words in the previous story, *STOP* the Reading Assessment here.

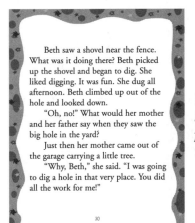

Beth saw a shovel near the fence. What was it doing there? Beth picked up the shovel and began to dig. She liked digging. It was fun. She dug all afternoon. Beth climbed up out of the hole and looked down.

"Oh, no!" What would her mother and her father say when they saw the big hole in the yard?

Just then her mother came out of the garage carrying a little tree.

"Why, Beth," she said. "I was going to dig a hole in that very place. You did all the work for me!"

30

Use assessment booklet page 30 for questions 13–15.

13. **Use page 30.** If your child stopped at fewer than 5 words in the above story, ask, *Can you read this story?* Again, supply a word if necessary. Circle the words your child has difficulty reading.

    Beth saw a shovel near the fence. What was it doing there? Beth picked up the shovel and began to dig. She liked to dig. It was fun. She dug all afternoon. Beth climbed up out of the hole and looked down.

"Oh, no!" What would her mother and father say when they saw the big hole in the yard?

Just then her mother came out of the garage carrying a little tree.

"Why, Beth," she said, "I was going to dig a hole in that very place. You did all the work for me!"

___ None

14. What does your child do to figure out a word he or she doesn't know? Check all that apply.
    ___ Guesses based on context.
    ___ Sounds it out.
    ___ Skips the word and then goes back.
    ___ Knew all the words.

15. **Use page 30.** Can your child answer these questions? Check all **correct** answers.
    ___ A. *What did Beth do all afternoon?* (She dug.)
    ___ B. *Why did Beth keep digging?* (She thought it was fun.)
    ___ C. *How did Beth feel after she dug the hole? Why?* (She felt nervous or afraid. She was afraid her parents would be mad.)
    ___ D. *What will Beth's mother do with the hole?* (She will plant a tree in the hole.)
    ___ E. Tell about a time when you did something like Beth. (Check if your child gives a response to the question.)

16. Which passages can your child read fluently—in smooth, expressive phrases rather than choppy, individual words?
    ___ getting ready for school
    ___ Tom and cat
    ___ riding bikes
    ___ Beth digs

    Check any that apply:
    ___ Frequently stumbles or stops to figure out words.
    ___ Generally reads word by word rather than in phrases.
    ___ Generally reads fluently but sometimes loses her place between lines.
    ___ Consistently reads fluently.

Assessment Guide

This assessment guide will tell you what the data you've collected on the Parent Observation Pages means. It will also direct you to the activity sections in this book that are most appropriate for your first grader.

Math Assessment

Mathematics is not simply learning to do computations (addition, subtraction, multiplication, etc.) in math workbooks. It is learning how to use math and mathematical ideas to solve problems in the real world. All children, even first graders, are introduced to overlapping strands of mathematical content. Those strands are *number, measurement, geometry, patterns and functions, probability and statistics, and logic.* These may sound like subjects that you took (or avoided) in high school. But because they make up the foundation of mathematical understanding, they are now introduced to young children through meaningful, concrete problem-solving activities.

Assessing these skills goes beyond marking answers right or wrong. To find out how your child is really doing in math, you must watch carefully as he or she goes about the business of solving a problem. The questions on the Parent Observation Pages will help you begin a habit of close observation so that you can help your child learn the mathematical thinking that today's world demands.

Question 1

This question measures your child's ability to name the basic shapes. Recognizing similarities and differences in shapes sets a foundation for mathematical thinking and helps children to see differences in other symbols such as letters and numbers. If your child could use practice in naming all four shapes, see Geometry, page 123.

Question 2

Sorting and classifying are skills relevant to every area of mathematics. Asking children to come up with their own rules for sorting helps them to recognize that problems can have many attributes, and therefore more than one solution. By the end of first grade your child should be able to come up with more than one way of classifying objects with two or more attributes (design, shape). If your child could use additional practice in sorting, see Sorting and Classifying, page 126.

Questions 3 and 4

Your child will probably spend a good deal of time this year working with patterns. Our number system is based on patterns. Working with patterns will help your child to have a better understanding of number and a stronger ability to solve problems. If your child could not complete the pattern in the first two rows or could not extend the pattern in the third, see Patterns, page 127, for ways to teach this concept.

Question 5

You want your child to be able to create a pattern and to develop the flexibility and creative thinking skills to construct more than one. If your child could not come up with more than one type of pattern—for instance, ABAB (yellow, green, yellow, green)—see Patterns, page 127.

Questions 6 and 7

These questions determine whether or not your child has the ability to conserve quantity. When a child has acquired conservation, he or she has the maturity to know how numbers work and can no longer be fooled by appearances. Re-counting the squares (using fingers or mentally) after you have stretched them out indicates that your child doesn't realize that changing the *position* of the squares does not alter the *number* of squares. *Conservation is not a skill that can be taught.* Just like first steps and the loss of baby teeth, a command of this concept will come. If your child has not shown an understanding of conservation, you will want to spend time working with concrete materials rather than with symbolic numbers. Experience and maturation go hand in hand with mathematical thinking.

In question 6 it is reasonable for your child to point with a finger while counting. This demonstrates a growing understanding of one-one correspondence. If your child was unable to count the number of squares correctly, see Number, page 130.

In question 7, if your child did not automatically say "Five," help him or her to become more experienced with number by doing the concrete activities in the Number section, page 130.

Question 8

A child who has had a good deal of practice with numbers will be able to answer this question without counting the squares from 1 to 7. If your child did not answer "Seven" automatically, see Number, page 130, and Addition and Subtraction, page 143.

Questions 9 and 10

These questions assess your child's ability to determine the missing part when shown one part—an important concept for both addition and subtraction. If your child had difficulty with either of these questions, see Number, page 130, and Addition and Subtraction, page 143.

Question 11

First graders need to be able to identify the number symbols before they can do paper-and-pencil computation. If your child needs more help in recognizing number symbols, see Number, page 130. Please note, however, that many first graders have difficulty distinguishing between 5 and 2 and 6 and 9, especially on a digital device like a clock or a calculator. As mentioned earlier, letter and number reversals are common in first grade and not a cause for concern. If your child asked, "Is this a two or a five?" chances are he or she does not need further practice in recognizing numbers. Time will do the trick.

Question 12

Children often appear quite precocious while counting by rote. This question determines whether or not your child can identify number symbols in the correct order. If your child had difficulty, see Number, page 130.

Question 13

By the end of first grade your child should be able to count to 100. If your child requires help with this skill, see Number, page 130.

Questions 14 to16

These questions evaluate your child's symbolic understanding of numbers greater than 10 and of place value. Place value is a difficult skill for children to learn, and in most schools it is not formally taught until the *end* of the first grade. If your child could use some help in identifying and understanding larger numbers, see Place Value, page 155.

Question 17

Skip-counting is fun, and it's a necessary skill. Children usually learn to skip-count by 10s, then 5s, and, by the end of first grade, by 2s. If your child can use some help in this area, see Skip-Counting, page 135.

Question 18

By the middle of the first grade year your child should know the names of coins. To help your child distinguish between coins and identify them by name, see Money, page 140.

Questions 19 and 20

By the end of first grade your child should know the values of the coins and be able to add small denominations. If your child could not identify the value of the coins or add them correctly, see Money, page 140.

Question 21

By the end of first grade your child should be able to read an analog clock to the hour and the half hour. If you would like to give your child more practice in this skill, see Time, page 142.

Questions 22 and 23

Measuring in nonconventional units (blocks, handprints, shoes) helps your child gain an understanding of the concept of measurement. Measuring in conventional units (inches, feet, and possibly metric units) is a life-skill application of the concept. If your child had difficulty with either of these questions, notice if he or she made any of these common errors:

- Began measuring from the wrong spot.
- Did not know where to stop measuring.
- Did not line the squares up so they were touching.
- Did not know how to read a ruler.

In some schools, measuring to the inch is a skill required in first grade. In other schools, mastery is not expected until second grade. If you would like to give your child additional practice in measuring, see Measurement, page 138.

Questions 24 to 26

The ability to estimate is an important mathematical skill. In fact, it's the skill we use most often in our daily lives. Estimating helps children to solve problems and to check their answers for accuracy. Practicing estimating also gives first graders a far better understanding of numbers. If your child had difficulty making reasonable estimates, see Number, page 130, and Estimating, page 137.

Questions 27 and 28

Solving word problems helps children apply math to their everyday lives. If your child made an error, try to determine if it was a computation error. If so, or if your child had difficulty figuring out *how* to solve the problem, you might want to see the activities listed in Addition and Subtraction, page 143. What strategies did your first grader use? He or she should be comfortable with at least two of the strategies listed. To strengthen your child's problem-solving abilities, see Word Problems, page 146.

Questions 29 and 30

Although this problem can be considered a multiplication problem, first graders who have developed a range of problem-solving strategies will find a way to work it out. If your child was able to answer questions 27 and 28 but not this question, see Word Problems, page 146. If your child was able to solve this problem and is comfortable using at least two strategies, you may want to investigate the activities in Math Enrichment, page 157.

Questions 31 to 34

Before your child adds and subtracts symbolically, with printed numbers, he or she should have plenty of practice using concrete manipulatives. For ideas on how to give your child the appropriate experiences, see Addition and Subtraction, page 143.

In questions 31 and 32, problems *a* and *b* measure your child's ability to add numbers to 10. Initially children use objects or draw pictures to solve these problems. Around midyear, however, as they become more proficient in number work, they should be able to solve these problems mentally by using a number of different strategies. To help your child develop these skills, see Addition and Subtraction, page 143, and Addition Strategies, page 148.

Problems *c* and *d* measure your child's ability to add numbers to 20. By the end of the first grade year, children should have developed several strategies for solving these math problems. To support and strengthen your child's work in this area, see Addition Strategies, page 148.

Problems *e* and *f* measure your child's ability to add and subtract two-digit numbers. This skill is usually introduced at the end of first grade. If your child demonstrates a strong understanding of adding numbers to 20 and is ready to tackle two-digit numbers, see Place Value, page 155. If your child answered all of these questions with ease, see Math Enrichment, page 157.

In questions 33 and 34, problems *a* and *b* measure your child's ability to subtract numbers below 10. Again, when introduced to subtraction, children use objects or draw pictures to solve problems. As they progress, they should be able to solve these problems mentally by using a number of different strategies. For more support in this skill, see Addition and Subtraction, page 143 and Subtraction Strategies, page 152.

Problems *c* and *d* measure your child's ability to subtract numbers below 20. Your child should be comfortable using more than two strategies to solve these problems. To provide more support in this skill, see Subtraction Strategies, page 152.

Problems *e* and *f* measure your child's ability to add and subtract two-digit numbers. This skill is usually introduced at the end of first grade. If your child demonstrates a strong understanding of subtracting numbers below 20 and is ready to tackle two-digit numbers, see Place Value, page 155. If he answered all of these questions with ease, see Math Enrichment, page 157.

In first grade, children develop a mathematical foundation to build on throughout their school years and beyond. Now is the time to encourage flexible thinking, strategies for problem-solving, and a love of mathematics. Even if your child seemed to have no difficulty with the questions on this assessment, you may want to skim the book for activities that will reinforce and expand his understanding. Feel free to adapt these exercises to meet the needs of your child. And be sure to read Math Enrichment, page 157.

Writing Assessment

Writing, like speaking, is developmental. Just as your child went through stages of language development—playing with sounds, babbling, one-word approximations such as "dada" for "daddy," singular words, and two-word sentences—she will also go through stages of writing development. This complex but predictable process is described in detail beginning on page 104. While reading the Writing Exercises chapter you will be able to determine where your child is developmentally and how you can best support her growth. By helping her become a better writer, you will be helping her to become a better reader as well.

Reading Assessment

Ask anyone what the first grade year in school is all about and the person will respond, "Learning to read." Just as you anxiously awaited your child's first tooth, first step, first word, you will now anticipate the moment when your child will perceive meaning in a string of letters and in strands of words.

But reading is not a skill that is mastered in a few weeks or even a few months. It is, instead, a process that begins in infancy and continues throughout the school years. It is a combination of skills, including decoding print (what does this word say?), vocabulary development (what does this word mean?), and comprehension (how well do I understand what I am reading?).

You may remember the way in which you were taught to read. Perhaps you were taught letter combinations and told to sound the word out (the phonics approach). Or perhaps you memorized familiar words from flash cards (the whole-word, or look-say, approach). Many teaching methods have been touted over the years. Fortunately, educators now realize that proficient readers use a number of different methods of making sense of print, and that children are best served when taught a range of strategies. These strategies include:

- Making predictions based on what the child knows
- Using clues from the pictures
- Using the context to determine the meanings of new words
- Using letter sounds to decode words
- Recognizing words by sight

The Assessment Guide will help you determine what reading skills your child has already acquired and what strategies you may want to work on next.

Questions 1 and 2

Your first grader should be able to name all of the uppercase and lowercase letters. To help your child learn letter names, see Identifying Letters, page 63.

Question 3

Learning letter sounds is essential to learning to read and write. If your child had difficulty naming some or all of the letter sounds, see Letter Sounds, 66. Please note that some children may have difficulty telling the sounds of letters in isolation. In other words, they cannot tell you the sound the letter *b* makes when it stands alone, but they can identify a word that begins with *b*. If your child has difficulty naming the sounds, try asking, *Can you tell me a word that begins with this letter?*

Question 4

These words contain the vowels *a, e, i, o,* and *u.* Differentiating between short vowels is a difficult skill for most six- to seven-year-olds, and mastery is not expected until the end of first grade or even during the second grade. If your child could identify the letter sounds in question 3 and two or more of these words, you might want to begin an introduction to short vowels. If so, see Letter Sounds, page 66, for suggestions.

Question 5

Beginning readers learn to use picture clues in combination with initial letter sounds to guess what words say. (Highly predictable stories such as this one support beginning readers.) If your child had difficulty reading this story, see Prediction, page 75, and Letter Sounds, page 66.

Question 6

This question asks your child to make a prediction based on what would make sense within the story pattern. If your child was unwilling to venture a guess or did not give a response that matched the story pattern, see Prediction, page 75.

Question 7

Some of the words in this reading passage are sight words (frequently used words that should be instantly recognized), others are words that can be successfully decoded (sounded out), and still others are words whose meaning can be determined from the context (the meaning of the text). See Sight Words, page 70, if your child had difficulty with any of these words: *was, on, his, way, he, saw, in, a, I, will, you, said, up, the, down, climbed, you,* or *are.* If your child had difficulty with any of these words: *Tom, home, cat, tree, help,* or *jumped,* see Letter Sounds, page 66; Phonics, page 77; and Identifying New Words, page 87.

Question 8

This question will help you determine which strategies your child is using to decode words. She should be using two or more. If she is relying on one strategy, or if the strategies she is using don't seem to be working, see Identifying New Words, page 87. You can also support your child's learning by determining which strategies she is not using and by turning to the appropriate exercises: If she does not attempt to sound out words, see Phonics, page 77. If your child does not use picture clues or does not make guesses based on meaning, see Prediction, page 75. If she could read this passage with ease, go on. Later passages will help you to record strategies.

Question 9

These questions help you to determine whether or not your child understands what he reads.

Questions A and B check your child's ability to recall what is stated in the text.

Question C asks your child to retell the ending in sequence.

Question D encourages your child to draw a conclusion using information from the story.

Question E encourages your child to use critical thinking skills to synthesize the information in the text and apply it to his own life.

If your child could read the words but had difficulty answering any of these questions, see Reading Comprehension, page 88. If your child particularly enjoyed answering question D, see Reading and Writing Enrichment, page 117 for activities that support and extend your child's reading and writing.

Question 10

If your child had difficulty with any of these words—*and, like, their, they, can, them, front, of, would, into, but, are, too,* or *busy*—see Sight Words, page 70. If she had difficulty with any of these words—*Mike, Pam, ride, bikes, park, sidewalk, house, town, need, wait, until, older, streets, going*—see Phonics, page 77, and Identifying New Words, page 87.

Question 11

This question gives you another opportunity to learn what your child does when she comes to an unknown word. If she seems to be using just one strategy, or if she has not tried skipping a word and coming back to it later, see Identifying New Words, page 87. If your child does not use the strategy of sounding words out, see Phonics, page 77. If she does not make guesses based on meaning, see Prediction, 75.

Question 12

These questions help you to determine whether or not your child understands what she reads.

Questions A and B ask your child to recall events from the story.

Question C checks your child's understanding of the vocabulary.

Question D requires your child to contrast and compare.

If your child read the text, but could not answer one or more of the questions, see Reading Comprehension, page 88. If your child particularly enjoyed answering question D, see Reading and Writing Enrichment, page 117.

Questions 13 and 14

Note which words cause your child difficulty and what he or she does when faced with an unknown word. If your child is using the same strategy over and over, or if the strategy she is using isn't working, see Identifying New Words, page 87; Prediction, page 75; or Phonics, page 77. If your child could read this passage with relative ease, see Reading and Writing Enrichment, page 117.

Question 15

Here is another opportunity to check your child's comprehension.

Questions A and B ask your child to recall events from the story.

Questions C and D invite your child to read between the lines, or infer, in order to figure out how Beth is feeling, based on information from the story.

Question E asks your child to analyze and apply the information in the story to make a new connection.

If your child had difficulty with one or more of these questions, see Reading Comprehension, page 88. If your child could read this selection with relative ease, see Reading and Writing Enrichment, page 117.

Question 16

If your child is still reading slowly, word by word, or having trouble keeping his place, see Reading Fluency, page 101.

If your child could read all of the words in this passage, you may want to repeat this activity using literature from home or the library. Choose a book that is slightly more difficult than the books your child is accustomed to. Or you could discuss this question with your child's teacher.

Reading Exercises

Identifying Letters

The ability to identify letters is measured by questions 1 and 2 in the Reading Assessment.

By the time your child has reached first grade, he should be able to identify most of the uppercase and lowercase letters accurately, with the exception of *b* and *d* or *p*, *g* and *q*, which are still likely to be confused. As mentioned earlier, reversing these letters is normal at the age of six and does not usually signal dyslexia or other reading problems. In all probability, your child will stop reversing letters by the age of seven. However, if your child is constantly asking, "which way is b and which way is d?" you might want to offer this first grade trick:

Print the word "bed" in large letters on a piece of paper. Have your child hold up his two pointer fingers and connect his two thumbs as shown in the diagram and place them on the word. Show her how her thumbs point out the direction the circle should go when writing a *b* or a *d*. When she is writing a word, and needs reminding which is the *b* and which is the *d*, have her make a "bed" with her hands.

It is also natural for a child to forget the names of letters that are rarely used such as *q*, *x*, and *z*. If your first grader missed a few, here are some activities to help him remember these letters and their names:

HAVE FIVE MINUTES?

➤Go on a letter hunt. See how many toughies such as *q*, *z*, or *v* your child can find in newspaper or magazine advertisements or in favorite books.

➤Let your child play with a gob of shaving cream on a table or counter. After he has played with it a bit, have him write letters in it. Shaving cream is easy to wipe up, leaving a surface that's cleaner than when you started!

➤Using chalk, draw one large letter at a time on the sidewalk or driveway. Have your child "walk" the letter, repeating its name over and over. To make the activity more interesting, ask your child to walk like a robot, a skater, a dinosaur, or a giant.

➤Draw letters on your child's back with your finger. Ask your first grader to guess the letter you are making. Then reverse roles.

➤Give your child a flashlight and invite him to make letters on the ceiling of a darkened room.

➤Chant letters. Take turns choosing one letter and writing it in uppercase and lowercase in a pattern—for instance, P p p P p p P p p, or L L L l l l L L L l l l. Say the letters aloud using a high-pitched voice for uppercase letters and a low-pitched voice for lowercase ones.

HAVE MORE TIME?

➤Go to your local library and find a number of different alphabet books. Ask your child to find letters in the different books. Then encourage him to compare the letters and the choice of objects illustrated. You might want to suggest that your first grader make his own alphabet book when you get home.

➤Allow your child to write letters in chocolate pudding!

➤Make cookies or pretzels shaped like letters. Here is an easy pretzel recipe to follow:
    1 pkg. active dry yeast
    ½ cup warm water
    1 tablespoon sugar

1 teaspoon salt
4 cups flour
1 egg
Coarse salt

    With your child, dissolve the yeast in the water. Add the next three ingredients and knead the dough until smooth. Form letters on slightly greased cookie sheet. Then brush with beaten egg and sprinkle with salt. Bake for 12 minutes at 425°F.

If your child has been in a preschool or kindergarten program where letters have been repeatedly introduced, but still does not recognize them by name, you will want to make an appointment to talk to his teacher. He may have a problem with visual perception or a problem with name recall that needs to be addressed. He may also qualify for in-school educational tutoring. In the meantime, you might want to help him strengthen his visual perception. Here are a few ways:

HAVE FIVE MINUTES?

➤ Cut a greeting-card picture or calendar picture into several large pieces. Have your child put the picture back together.

➤ Trace around several objects such as a block, a carrot, and a marble. Ask your child to match the objects to the tracings.

HAVE MORE TIME?

➤ Go on a shape walk. Look for lines and circles in the architecture and nature you pass. Find repeated patterns. Whenever possible, have your child point out a similar shape to the one that you've pointed out.

➤ Choose the letters that your child has difficulty remembering. Write them on two sets of cards. Then turn the cards over and play a game of Concentration. Players take turns flipping two cards over at a time. If the cards match, the player gets to keep them. It the cards do not match, they are turned back over. This is a time-honored classroom game that helps children with both visual discrimination and memory.

➤ Play Go Fish, Crazy Eights, or Old Maid with your child.

➤ Invest in a couple of commercial puzzles if your child does not have any. (These can be frequently purchased at yard sales.) You will probably want to begin with puzzles composed of fewer than twenty pieces and build up to more difficult puzzles.

Letter Sounds

The ability to identify letter sounds is measured by questions 3, 4, 5, and 7 on the Reading Assessment.

Identifying the sounds of letters is one of the most important skills taught in first grade. Without sound identification, children cannot use the strategy known as phonics.

How can a mere six-year-old learn the sounds of twenty-six letters, including *c* and *g*, which have two sounds each? Fortunately, if your child can name the letters, she is on her way to recognizing their sounds. Say the consonants *s*, *t*, and *r*. The letter names are close to the sounds they represent. For this reason many of the consonants and all of the long vowels (*a* as in "cake," *e* as in "Pete," *i* as in "kite," *o* as in "home," and *u* as in "flute") are easier to learn than the short vowel sounds (*a* as in "cat," *e* as in "bed," etc.).

Don't be too concerned if your first grader cannot name all of the short vowel sounds. These require a more sophisticated ability to differentiate between closely related sounds and a more sophisticated form of memorization. It is quite possible for your child to begin reading with the use of other strategies before he has mastered all of the letter sounds.

When introducing or practicing letter sounds with your child, begin with oral games. Try not to extend the sounds of letters. For example, when saying the sound of b, do not add a "uh" sound. The sounds should be short and clipped. Learning the sounds accurately, without stretching them out, will help her to blend sounds to decode words when reading.

After your child has experienced success with informal games, work with printed letters.

HAVE FIVE MINUTES?

ORAL GAMES:

➤ Say, "Can you tell me something that begins with the same sound as 'ball'?" Have your child name as many things as she can think of. First graders love a challenge, so after she's named a few, say: "I'm sure you can't possibly think of one more."

➤ Make up zany sentences in which every word has the same beginning sound. For instance: "Little Laura Lilly liked licking lollipops." Ask your child to identify the beginning sound. Then invite her to make up another sentence with lots of the same sounds. (In third or fourth grade, she'll learn that this is called alliteration.)

➤ Sing familiar nursery rhymes by changing the first consonants of the words. For instance you might sing: "Tonden Tridge is talling town," or "Bumpty Bumpty bat on a ball." Have your child identify the letter you used.

➤ Play I Spy. Say "I spy something on the floor that begins with the same sound as 'toaster.'" When she has found that object, ask a similar question using the letter name: "I spy something on the counter that begins with the letter *t*." If your child chooses the right sound but the wrong beginning letter—if, for instance, when looking for words that begin with *s*, she says "cereal"—say, "'Cereal' does begin with the /s/ sound." You need not correct her, since its her job to focus on sounds at this time.

➤ Play Clap, Stomp. Ask your child to listen for a letter such as *k*. Tell her to clap if the *k* sound is at the beginning of the word and to stomp if it's at the end of the word. Then name a list of words such as *kite, back, trick,* and *kangaroo*.

➤ Sing "My Bonnie Lies Over the Ocean." Whenever your child hears a *b* sound, have her stand up. When she hears the next *b*, have her sit down. Continue in this way (with much laughter) until the song is over.

WORKING WITH LETTERS:

➤ Family names tend to be among the first words your child reads. Write the names such as *Mommy, Grammy,* and *David* on separate sheets of paper. Invite your first grader to draw pictures of other objects on each sheet of paper that begin with the same letter as the name.

➤ Place signs or labels around your child's room (Post-it Notes are ideal for this purpose). Each night ask, "Which word would you like tonight?" Your child might suggest "window," "chair," or her favorite toy dog, "Mr. Rover." Write the word in lowercase letters and help your child fasten the labels to the objects.

After you have placed a number of labels, play games with them. "I see two things that begin with the letter *b*," or "I see something that begins with the same sound as Mr. Rover."

HAVE MORE TIME?

ORAL GAMES:

➤ Remember the "I'm going on a picnic" game you used to play on long car rides? This is a great game for practicing letter sounds and improving memory. The first person begins by saying, "I'm going on a picnic, and in my basket I'll pack a [something that begins with *a*]. The next player repeats what the first player has said and adds an item that begins with *b*. Play continues until you've reached the letter *z*. (If your child has difficulty repeating objects that have been packed, concentrate on adding new items only. You can help her keep her place in the alphabet.)

➤ Believe it or not, encouraging your child to write is one of the best ways to help her learn and remember the sounds of the letters. Suggest that she write a list, a note, or a label for a picture using her own spelling. (Read the discussion of practice spelling on pages 27–28 if you haven't already.)

When your child begins writing, she may ask, "How do you spell 'hat'?" Instead of providing your child with the letters, ask, "What sounds do you hear in the word 'hat'? " Your child will be reinforcing her knowledge as she records the sounds she hears.

Let your child know that you would rather not spell a word for her, but you will be happy to supply a sound. In other words, encourage your child to ask what makes the /h/ sound, in which case you say the letter *h*. The more your child writes, the more sounds she will need, the more questions she will ask, and the more she will learn (and remember).

Remember that children may not hear *all* the sounds in a word at this stage. It's quite possible that your child will hear and identify only the beginning sound or the beginning and ending sounds in each word. Praise her for identifying these sounds, without any mention of missing letters.

Again, if you've practiced and practiced the sounds of the letters and your child is still having difficulty, you'll want to speak to her teacher about auditory

To Holly
I wish we could play today.

A man is picking apples at an apple orchard.

testing. A child who has had frequent ear infections, hearing loss, or difficulty pronouncing words correctly may need speech therapy to help her hear isolated sounds effectively.

Instead of focusing on letter sounds to the point of frustration, try some of these activities instead:

HAVE FIVE MINUTES?

➤ Go on a sound walk. How many sounds can your child hear and identify?

➤ Have your child close her eyes. Walk around the room saying the word "beep," softly. After five beeps, have your child point to where she thinks you are in the room.

➤ Have your child close her eyes while you make a sound—by shaking a marble tin, for example, or by running a toy car across the floor or stamping your feet. Have your child guess how you made the sound. Then switch roles.

➤ Place a different amount of water in each of five glasses. Have your child play musical sounds by lightly tapping the rim of each glass with a spoon. Ask her which glass makes the highest sound? Which makes the lowest sound? If you are capable, hum one of the sounds and have your child try to match it.

➤ Record common sounds on a tape recorder. Then have your child listen to the sounds and identify them. Discovery Toys has a bingo game entitled *Hear the World,* in which children identify sounds on a cassette tape and place a bingo chip on the matching picture. You may have a Discovery Toy representative in your town, or you can call 1-800-426-4777.

Sight Words

The ability to read sight words is measured by questions 7 and 10 on the Reading Assessment.

As you read this sentence, you do not need to stop and figure out each separate word. You have memorized all of these words and can recall them instantly by sight. That is what a sight word is: a word that can be immediately known just by glancing at the configuration of letters. In order for your child to read fluently, he needs to acquire a growing list of words that he recognizes effortlessly.

Teachers normally concentrate on two categories of sight words. The first category is made up of frequently used words. Although there are nearly half a million words in the English language, only thirty-three words account for one-third of our written material! If you can help your child memorize these thirty-three words, he will be on his way to reading:

a	of	and	that	he	the	I
to	in	was	it	all	had	said
as	have	so	at	him	they	be
his	we	but	not	with	are	on
you	for	one	she	her		

(For a list of the most frequently used words in children's literature, please see page 175 in the appendix.)

The second category of sight words is composed of words that cannot be decoded in isolation. If your child knows letter sounds, she can probably read the word "in" by blending the letter sounds. She cannot do this, however, with the word "said," which follows none of the rules of phonics. Because it occurs frequently, and because it cannot be decoded, "said" is a good word to teach your child in the early stages of reading.

Chances are your child already has a large store of complex sight words. He may be able to read "Dunkin' Donuts," "Legos," "Stop," and other words that he sees frequently. Know that recognizing printed words in the environment is an important and crucial part of learning to read. Respond enthusiastically the next time your first grader reads a street sign, a newspaper advertisement, or a cereal box. By reinforcing his efforts to read words in the larger world, you will help him build up an "I can" attitude that will carry over when it comes time to recognize words in books.

Although it's tempting to make flash cards of sight words, drilling your child in this way adds unnecessary pressure and quickly zaps the joy from learning to read. In fact, if your child is having difficulty retaining sight words, he will probably not benefit from the flash card approach. Instead, help him learn sight words in the context of real reading and writing. Here are some ways in which you can build your child's sight vocabulary while keeping a sense of adventure and fun.

HAVE FIVE MINUTES?

➤ Surprise your child with frequent notes. Place a note under his cereal bowl, in his lunch box, or on his pillow. Your child will be motivated to read a note from you and will begin to see certain words repeated. In the following note there are eight frequently used words:

Dear Kyle,

    <u>Have</u> <u>a</u> fun day at school. <u>I</u> can't wait <u>to</u> <u>see</u> <u>you</u> <u>in</u> <u>the</u> play tonight!

Love,
Dad

➤ To give your child some additional assistance, you might make a rebus note. In a rebus, some of the words appear as pictures. Here is the same note written in rebus form:

Dear Kyle,

Have a fun day at  .

I can't wait to see you in the  tonight!

Love,
Dad

➤ Save flyers, such as pizza advertisements or sale announcements, to give to your first grader in the 4:00 to 6:00 P.M. meltdown hours. Suggest that he circle every word he knows. Remember to get just as excited about his circles around "Pizza Hut" as you do around words such as "you" and "take." This is also a great activity to do in restaurants that supply paper take-out menus.

➤ Have your child cut out words he recognizes from newspapers, magazines, and flyers and make a word collage by randomly gluing them onto paper. Post the collage in his room or on the refrigerator. Have him add to his collage as his sight vocabulary grows.

➤ Suggest that your child begin a word collection. Each day, perhaps first thing in the morning, write one word on an index card. It can be a word that he wants to learn, a word from a book that he is attempting to read, or a word that he writes regularly. Don't limit the size or nature of these words. A child can learn to recognize a word such as "hamster," "rainbow," or "tornado" if it pertains to his interests or if he frequently uses it. Write the word on an index card and have him store the cards in a shoe box or on a metal ring. From time to time let him practice reading his collection to you.

➤ Invite your child to dictate a story to you. As he watches you write down the sentences, he will see how the words look. He may want to read the story back to you.

HAVE MORE TIME?

➤ Investigate the little books known as emergent readers at your local library. Rookie Readers is one of the oldest and most familiar series; other popular series are listed below. These stories are written with just a few words, are highly repetitive, and provide lots of support in the illustrations. You may want to read the story to your child first, then encourage him to read it a second time on his own. Don't worry that these books are easy to memorize. In learning these books by heart, your child is building his store of sight words. When he is proficient at reading a story, have him read it to his sitter, his grandmother, his goldfish.

Here are some emergent reader series you can look for at your library and at the bookstore (most are paperbacks and priced under $4.00):

GoodYear Books, Scott Foresman Co. These are highly repetitive and predictable. Your child will no doubt begin to identify himself as a successful reader while attempting the books in this series. Although they're easy to memorize, they reinforce basic sight words and help your child to read for meaning. There are three levels of books in this series for reading progression.

My First Readers, Children's Press. Each book in this series uses twenty words over and over, helping to build your child's sight vocabulary. The titles are slightly less repetitive and predictable than the GoodYear Books.

Bank Street Ready to Read, Bantam Books (Byron Press). There are three levels and many titles in this series. You are bound to find books that meet your child's interests—snakes and fairy tales, for example—as well as support his beginning skills. Some of the Bank Street books are written in rebus style.

Get Ready, Get Set, Read Books, Barron's. These books are built around phonetic word families. For instance, one book may use *ed* words such as *Ted, Ed, bed, sled, fed*. Because the vocabulary is so highly controlled, the stories can hardly be called good literature. A too heavy dose of this type of book might give your child the message that reading is anything but exciting. But read sparingly, these books do serve a purpose.

School Zone Start to Read Series, School Zone Publishing Co. Another series of phonetic readers with three levels to choose from. Again, try not to purchase books of this variety alone. The stilted language prompted one first grader to say, "A grown-up wrote this?"

Hello Reader! Scholastic. Your child may bring home book club order forms with this series. This is how Scholastic divides the books into four levels:

Level	Grade	Ages
1	Preschool–Grade 1	3–6
2	Kindergarten–Grade 2	5–7
3	Grades 1–2	6–8
4	Grades 2–3	7–9

Don't worry if you choose a book that is too difficult for your child. You can always do shared reading in which you read most of the book but pause when you come to a word your child can read, predict, or sound out successfully.

There are also some tried-and-true picture books that have very consistent and simple structures which will not only reinforce sight words but also help your child to feel like a truly competent reader: *Brown Bear, Brown Bear, What Do You See?*, by Bill Martin Jr., Holt, 1984; *Cat on the Mat*, by Brian Wildsmith, Oxford, 1982 *(often the first book a child will read on his own); Chick and the Duckling* by Mirra Ginsburg, Macmillan, 1972; *I Went Walking* by Sue Williams, Harcourt, 1990.

➤ You may want to suggest that your child write her own little book using the pattern from an existing book. Consider the pattern from Bill Martin's soon to be classic, *Brown Bear Brown Bear:*

"Brown Bear, Brown Bear, What do you see?"

"I see a red bird looking at me."

"Redbird, redbird, What do you see?"

"I see a yellow duck looking at me."

Your child can write a book of his own, reinforcing his knowledge of many frequently used words:

"Orange truck, orange truck, What do you see?"

"I see a yellow bulldozer looking at me."

➤ Highly predictable books that repeat a refrain: "I think I can, I think I can, I think I can"—also help your child to retain sight words. For a list of predictable books and suggestions on how to use them, see Prediction, opposite page.

➤ Create a simple scavenger hunt. Print single words on index cards or slips of paper and place them strategically around your house. For instance, you might hand your child a card that reads *"bed."* He reads the word and goes racing off to the beds to find the next word: *"door."* There are several possible places to look for these cards, but that adds fun and excitement to the game. Plant a treat or a card that reads, *"You win!"* to signal the end of the hunt.

➤ First graders enjoy learning about themselves. Help your child write and illustrate a book about himself using many of the sight words. Here are a few sentences your first grader could complete:

My name is _____.

These are the people in my family: _____.

This is my mother. She is _____.

This is my father. He is _____.

Here are my pets. They can _____.

I am happy that _____.

Encourage your child to read his finished book to others.

➤ Make a fortuneteller. Here's how:

1. Cut a square from a sheet of 8½" x 11" paper by folding the upper right-hand corner down as shown, and cutting off the excess paper at the bottom.

2. Open the square and fold it diagonally in half the other way. Open the square again.

3. Now fold each of the corners into the center as shown.

4. Turn the paper over. Fold the corners into the center point again.

5. Write the names of colors on each of the eight small triangles. On the back of each triangle (open the flap) write a fortune such as "Your wish will come true," or "You will make a new friend." (Use frequently used words.)

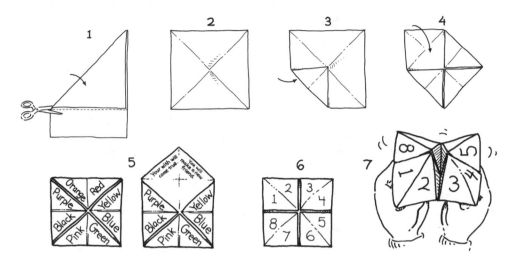

6. Turn the paper over. Write the numbers 1 to 8, one in each triangle.

7. With colors facing up, slip thumbs and pointer fingers into the numbered flaps underneath and pinch points together as shown.

8. Ask your child to pick a number. Open and close the fortuneteller, first in one direction, then the other, that number of times. Ask your child to pick a color. Open that color flap to read his fortune. No doubt your child will want to have all his friends try his fortuneteller, which will give him plenty of practice in reading sight words! As your child becomes more proficient in using the fortuneteller, have him write the names of the colors on the outside and the numbers on the inside. Your child can open and close the fortuneteller while spelling the color word chosen.

Prediction

The ability to use prediction is measured by questions 5, 6, 8, 11, 13, and 14 on the Reading Assessment.

You may remember your first grade teacher telling you not to guess when you came to an unknown word.

Guess what? Research disagrees. You want your child to be able to take risks in reading. You want her to become a confident guesser—not a wild, shoot-it-into-the-wind guesser but one who can make calculated predictions based on the information available.

A child who sees a sign on a door can use the following information to read the print: the door next to this door has a picture of a lady on the sign (context); this door has a picture and a sign that begins with an *m* and ends with an *n* (phonics).

Good readers are always thinking ahead, predicting what the text will say.

HAVE FIVE MINUTES?

➤ Before reading a book, have your child look at the cover and predict what the story will be about. Ask your child to tell you how she made the prediction. Halfway through the story, give her the opportunity to extend or change her prediction.

➤ Invite your child to predict what signs say as you ride in the car, shop, or visit places. Whenever possible, give credit for incorrect guesses. You might say, "I can see why you thought that sign over the door says 'Out.' Let's look at the first letters. What sounds do *e* and *x* make?" Remember, you want to encourage prediction, not discourage it. All suggestions should be honored.

➤ Read rhyming or patterned books and pause when you come to words your child can easily supply through prediction. Here are some recommended books that have either rhyming text or a repeating pattern:

Buzz, Buzz, Buzz, went Bumblebee, by Colin West, Candlewick

Caps for Sale, by Esphyr Slobodkina, Harper *(you probably remember this classic)*

Cock A Doodle Moo, by Bernard Most, Harcourt Brace

Elephants Swim, by Linda Capus Riley, Houghton Mifflin *(a nonfiction title with notes about each animal at the end)*

Fire! Fire! Said Mrs. McGuire, by Bill Martin Jr., Harcourt

Hush: A Thai Lullaby, by Minfong Ho, Orchard

In the Small, Small Pond, by Denise Fleming, Holt

Jump, Frog, Jump, by Robert Kalan, Greenwillow

My Little Sister Ate One Hare, by Bill Grossman, Crown *(a hilarious counting book)*

Noisy Nora, by Rosemary Wells, Dial

One Windy Wednesday, by Phillis Root, Candlewick

One Red Rooster, by Kathleen Sullivan Carroll, Houghton Mifflin

Over on the Farm, by Christopher Gunsen, Scholastic Press
Papa!, by Philippe Corentin, Chronicle
Rosie's Walk, by Pat Hutchins, Macmillan
The Biggest Horse I Ever Did See, by Susan Arkin Couture, HarperCollins
Tumble Bumble, by Felicia Bond, Front Street
Yo! Yes?, by Chris Raschka, Orchard
We're Going on a Bear Hunt, by Michael Rosen, Margaret K. McElderry

HAVE MORE TIME?

➤ Read a chapter book to your child. When you reach the cliff-hanger at the end of a chapter, have your child predict what will happen next.

Phonics

The ability to use phonics is measured by questions 7, 8, 10, 11, 13, and 14 on the Reading Assessment.

There are 110 phonics rules, but very few of them are applicable 100 percent of the time. This makes it mighty tempting to call that 800 number you heard on the radio or to send for your free trial of a guaranteed (albeit expensive) phonics program. Using a commercial phonics program isn't necessary, however, and sometimes causes more harm than good.

When teaching your child phonics, here are two points to remember.

➤ Phonics is just one of several reading strategies and should not dominate a child's learning time. If children are subjected to heavy doses of sounding out words in isolation—in other words decoding words in activity books or on cards and not in the stories—they may place too much emphasis on this one strategy. They may read word by word without fluency or attention to meaning. Which brings us to the next point.

➤ Reading for meaning is what reading is all about. If you teach your child a few basic phonics rules while sharing wonderful literature, you will be imparting worthwhile strategies and helping your child become hooked on books for life.

Here is a list of eight things you can do to help your child develop stronger skills in phonics (letter combinations) and phonemic awareness (sounds that letter combinations make):

1. Encourage your child to write, using practice spelling, often.
2. Play with rhymes.

3. Show your child how to blend letters to sound out words.
4. Teach the *h* digraphs: *ch, sh, th, wh, ph,* and *gh.*
5. Teach the silent *e* rule.
6. Teach the ending *ing.*
7. Explore long vowel combinations: *ea, ee, ai, ue.*
8. Explore syllabication.

Writing

One of the best ways to support your child in learning phonics is to encourage her to write often. When your child writes, and requests spellings, you can help her reconstruct our phonetic system. Here is a typical conversation between a parent and a first grader:

"Mom, how do you spell 'hope'?"

"What sounds do you hear?"

"*Huh.* What makes that sound?"

"The letter *h* makes that sound. What do you hear next?"

"The *o* sound. I know *o.*"

"Good. Write that down. What do you hear at the end of the word?"

"I hear *p.*"

"Now read the word back."

"H-o-p. It says 'hop.'"

"What do you need to make this word say 'hope'?"

"An *e!* I need silent *e* to make the *o* say its name."

"That's right. You wrote the word 'hope'!"

Instead of trying to memorize lists of arbitrary rules, this first grader is learning phonics because she *needs* the system. She is also engaging with her mother, creating a more emotionally meaningful learning experience—something that cannot happen with a series of tape-recorded messages and individual games. There is no doubt that she will have an easier time remembering the rules that she has helped construct.

The child who wrote "hope" already knows a good deal about letters and writing. She knows and *hears* the sounds of *o* and *p.* She knows the silent *e* rule. She can identify the *h* sound even though she cannot recall which letter makes that sound. Children do not begin at this point. When children begin to use practice spelling, they may hear only one or two letters of a word. In their writing, the words may not be separated by spaces, and vowels may not be used at all. To determine your child's developmental stage of writing, please read Writing Stages and Exercises, page 104.

If your child is already in the habit of asking you how to spell words, and if you have been providing the correct spelling, she may balk at your suggestion that she write the sounds she hears. After all, she knows there is a correct spelling, she knows you know it, and that's what she wants to write. But by supplying the correct spelling, you can slow her growth in understanding phonics and undermine her confidence as an independent writer. Tell her that she is ready to write the sounds *she* hears and praise her for every attempt. If, after she has written the word, she insists on knowing if it is right, praise her again for doing her own writing. Tell her that by writing the sounds she hears, she is teaching herself to read. Then point out which letters match the correct spelling. You might say, "Look! You heard the *h* and the *p!* That's splendid." Eventually, your child will be ready to revise her practice spelling so that it is correct. But for now you'll want to encourage risk-taking and a sense of accomplishment when learning how to build words.

HAVE FIVE MINUTES?

➤ Take the time to ask, "What sounds do you hear?" when your child asks for a spelling of a word.

➤ If your child knows only a few letter sounds or names of letters, she may answer your question, "What sounds do you hear?" by naming one of the letters in her repertoire:
"What sound do you hear in hope?"
"d"
"What sound do your hear in mat?"
"d"
If this is the case, tell your child to write that letter down. This will reinforce her early (and sincere) efforts. Then spend time doing the activities in Letter Sounds, page 66, to help her learn more consonant sounds.

➤ Model the process of building words. Write a list in front of your child. For instance, you might say: "I want to write the word 'macaroni.' Let's see. I hear the sound *m*." Chances are your child will quickly chime in with the letters she can identify.

➤ When you're on the phone and your child wants to interrupt, have her write you a note. Then excuse yourself from the conversation momentarily to respond to the note.

HAVE MORE TIME?

➤ Begin a dialogue journal. Buy a composition book or staple some sheets of paper together. Each day, encourage your child to write in the journal. Then borrow the book and write back. Do not correct your child's spelling. After all, it's the meaning of his words that is most important.

But do use the same (correctly spelled) words in your response that your child used. That way, he can see the correct spelling when he reads your letter. This is how children begin to understand the phonics system and adjust their own writing.

For a complete list of ways to spur your child's writing, see Writing Stages and Exercises, page 104.

Playing with rhymes

Rhyming words give children plenty of practice in learning word families. Here are two samples of word families:

ap: cap, gap, lap, map, nap, rap, sap, tap, chap, clap, slap, snap, trap

ook: book, cook, hook, look, nook, took, brook, crook, shook.

(For a list of word families see appendix, page 175.)

One word of caution. You'll want to closely monitor the rhyming work your child does to make sure that she is hearing the letter sounds correctly. If she thinks *"hit"* rhymes with *"hat"* or *"cap"* rhymes with *"cat"* help her to hear the differences.

HAVE FIVE MINUTES?

➤ Play Pass the Rhyme while you're waiting for the bus, the doctor, or the popcorn to finish popping. You say a short word such as *"fin."* Your child thinks of a rhyming word such as *"tin."* You say *"win."* Play back and forth until one of you cannot think of a rhyme. The one who is stumped thinks of a new word to pass.

When your child has become familiar with this game, write the rhyming words on a sheet of paper and pass it back and forth between you. Do not be concerned if your child misspells a rhyming word. For instance she may write *"hed"* to rhyme with *"bed."* Show the correct spelling and praise her for hearing the correct sounds.

➤ Give your child magnetic letters or print each letter on a small card. Challenge your child to build rhyming words. Say, for example, "Build a word that rhymes with 'hot'" or "Build a word that rhymes with 'toy.'"

➤ Read rhyming books; you will find a list of recommended books on pages 76–77. Pause when you come to a rhyming word and invite your child to supply it.

➤ Make up a rhyming message-of-the-day and post it on the refrigerator. Try to give hints about your first grader's day. You might write, "I have a hunch. You will love your _____" (lunch) *or* "Good luck today on your *math.* When you get home give Spot a _____" (bath).

At first you may need to read the message aloud and allow your child to fill in the missing word. Eventually she will be able to read and answer the notes on her own.

➤ Have your first grader create an imaginary shopping list. Write a simple word at the top of a sheet of paper. Tell your child she may pretend to buy anything that rhymes with the word at the top.

pat
Hat
Cat
rat
bat
mat
laundromat
Wildcat
acrobat

HAVE MORE TIME?

➤ Show your child how to make a rhyme tree. Draw a tree on a sheet of paper. Write a simple word on the trunk. Encourage your child to write rhyming words in circles at the ends of the tree branches. If your child is willing to take the activity one step further, have her write a poem using the rhyming words. (Honor your child's early attempts at poetry without making mechanical corrections. See Writing Stages and Exercises, page 104, for a discussion on how to respond to first drafts.)

My Mom threw her mop
She said, I'll be a cop
O.K. said my Pop
I gave a hop

Blending letters to sound out words

When children are asked to sound out a word, they often try to pronounce each letter separately and then put it all together at the end. So a child reading the word *problem* would say each letter sound separately and hope that the sounds made sense. This is not an easy or efficient way to decode.

Instead, teach your child to blend the sounds as she goes. Use your finger or a book mark to cover the letters that she hasn't come to. Blending the word *problem* is done in this way: /p/ /pr/ /pro/ /prob/ /probl/ /proble/ /problem/

Your child may get halfway and predict what the word says. If she is accurate, she is reading for meaning, and this is to be commended. If her predictions are not logical, she needs to be encouraged to slow down and blend the entire word.

HAVE FIVE MINUTES?

➤ When your child comes to an unknown word, sound it out for her by blending the letters slowly. Repeat this several times throughout a single sitting so she can hear how blending is done.

➤ Play a game in which you stretch out the letter sounds of a word for your child, then tell your child to say it fast. For example:
"G-r-ee-n."
"Green!"
"Tr-ai-l-er."
"Trailer!"
Now reverse roles.

HAVE MORE TIME?

➤ Gather a pile of small blocks. Ask, "How many sounds [sounds, not letters] do you hear in the word 'stick'?" Have your child choose a block for each sound she hears. For the word "stick," she would choose four blocks *(s-t-i-c-k)*.

Teaching the h digraphs

Digraphs are two letters that, when placed side by side, create a new sound. The digraphs are *sh, ch, th, wh, ph,* and *gh.* The following words contain digraphs (notice that *th* has two sounds):

chair	share	them	throw	when	phone
chin	shop	this	thing	where	photo
chomp	shell	there	thin	why	rough
church	ship	then	thumb	what	

➤ When reading to your child, point out words that contain digraphs. Tell your child the sound the two letters make when written together. Challenge your child to find other words in the book you're reading that have the same digraph.

➤ Teach your child tongue twisters such as "She sells seashells by the seashore," or "How much wood would a woodchuck chuck if a woodchuck could chuck wood?" Ask which two letters make the /sh/ sound? Which two letters make the /ch/ sound?

➤ Read the newspaper comics to your child. Then ask your child to point out the digraphs she sees at the beginning of words. Reread words with digraphs, pronouncing the digraph sound in a louder voice.

➤ Make up questions with one-word answers that have digraphs. For instance, "I'm thinking of a word that describes something you put on after your socks and begins with *sh*" (shoes). Or, "I'm thinking of a kind of ape whose name begins with *ch*" (chimp).

HAVE MORE TIME?

➤ Photocopy and cut out the cards on page 187 in the back of the book. Challenge your child to move the cards around to make words. How many can she make? (Answers: *ship, chip, whip, shin, chin, thin, chop, shop, chat, that, what.*) If your child suggests "whin" for "win," explain that the English language has many ways of spelling words, and that 'win' does not have an *h*. This may also be a good time to teach the sight word "what."

Digraph Cards	
ch	sh
wh	th
in	at
op	ip

The silent e rule

Here's the rule: When a word has a vowel, a consonant, and a final E *(tape, rope, line)*, the silent *e* makes the vowel say its name. This is one of our most frequently used rules.

HAVE FIVE MINUTES?

➤ Invent a story about the power of silent *e,* using three- and four-letter words that make new words when an *e* is added. For example: "Last night I saw a robbery taking place. The trusty silent *e* came along and turned my ordinary 'cap' into a 'cape.' With my cape, I had superhuman powers. I chased the robbers away."

Write the word "cap" and change it to "cape" as you tell the story. Here is a list of silent *e* words to draw from:

bit, bite	glob, globe	mad, made	rip, ripe	strip, stripe
can, cane	Jan, Jane	man, mane	rob, robe	tap, tape
cod, code	hat, hate	not, note	Sam, same	Tim, time
con, cone	hid, hide	pal, pale	scrap, scrape	tub, tube
fin, fine	hop, hope	pin, pine	slid, slide	twin, twine
fir, fire	kit, kite	plan, plane	slop, slope	win, wine

Invite your child to make up stories of his own that demonstrate the power of the silent *e.*

➤ Photocopy and cut out the cards on page 188 in the back of the book. Have your child read each word. Then have her add a silent *e* to each card and read the new words.

Silent "e" Cards			
bit	e	glob	e
can	e	mad	e
strip	e	hop	e
tap	e	rip	e
hat	e	not	e
hid	e	pal	e
scrap	e	tub	e
Pet	e	slid	e

➤When you're reading aloud to your child, point out words with a silent *e*. Put your hand over the *e* and ask, "How would you read this word without the *e*?" (The letters may not make up a real word. For instance, if you covered the *e* on *"blaze,"* the word remaining letters would read *"blaz."*) Then uncover the *e* and ask, "Now how do you read the word?"

➤Choose a book that your child is familiar with. When you come to a silent *e* word, such as *chase,* read it with the short vowel sound (*chas*). Let your child correct you: "No, that word is 'chase'!" Then let her convince you that the *e* makes the vowel say its name.

The -ing *ending*

To prevent your child from trying to sound out the *-ing* ending, which appears very frequently, have her practice looking at the three letters and pronouncing the *ing* sound.

HAVE FIVE MINUTES?

➤Write these words on a sheet of paper: *ring, ding, sing, ping, king, wing.* Tell your child the special sound that *-ing* makes. Then ask him to read the words on the paper. Instant success!

➤Using magnetic letters on the refrigerator, write the word *sing.* Then challenge your child to replace the first letter to make a new word. It's also fun to work with magnetic letters on a cookie sheet.

➤Here is a fun game to play while traveling in the car. One player suggests a setting such as the kitchen. Then each of the other players names actions that can be done in the kitchen with an *-ing* ending: baking, stirring, washing, cooking, frying. Play until no other actions can be recalled. The player who thinks of the last action gets to choose the next setting.

➤When your child comes to an *-ing* word while reading, frame the letters with your fingers and have her recall what sound the three letters make.

Long vowel combinations

You may want to teach your child this way to remember several long vowel combinations: "When two vowels go walking, the first one does the talking." Or when *ea, ee, ai, oa, ue* are together, the first vowel says its name and the second vowel is silent. Some combinations (*ou, oi,* and *oo*) are exceptions to this rule.

HAVE FIVE MINUTES?

➤ To help your child remember this rule, have her draw a letter picture. Have her choose a word that has the *ai, ea,* or *ee* combination. Then suggest she draw a silly picture of the letters in which the first vowel is being big, bold, and shouting; and the second vowel is being shy and quiet. Perhaps you can draw your own picture alongside hers.

➤ Read the book *Sheep in a Jeep* by Nancy Shaw (Houghton, 1986). This rollicking tale, which your child may be able to read on her own, is full of words that contain *ee* and *ea.* Point out the vowel combinations as you read.

➤ Using magnetic letters, make the *ea, ee,* and *ai* combinations. Have your child choose consonants to make words.

HAVE MORE TIME?

➤ Hang a large sheet of paper in your child's room. Every time you come across a word with two vowels in which the first one does the talking and the second one does the walking, have your child write the word on the "word wall." You may want to write the vowel combinations at the top and have your child list the words in five columns. See how many words you can find.

Exploring syllabication

Dividing words into segments helps children to decode words when reading. If you are familiar with syllabication you would likely divide the word "backpack" in this way: "back-pack." (Chances are you would be able to predict the word after reading back.) That is far more effective than trying to blend the letters *ckp* in the middle of this word.

HAVE FIVE MINUTES?

➤ Determine how many syllables each person in your family has in his or her name. As you and your child say a name, put up fingers to represent the syllables. How many syllables are in your last name?

➤ Invite your child to clap the number of syllables in the days of the week. You might use this chant:

Today is Monday (clap on "Mon" and "day").

Tomorrow is Tuesday (clap on "Tues" and "day").

The next day is Wednesday (clap on "wens" and "day").

The next day is . . .

After chanting and clapping, ask, "Can you name a day that has two syllables? Can you name a day that has three?" (Sat-ur-day).

HAVE MORE TIME?

➤ Give your child a pile of paper clips. Then say a word. Have your child choose a paper clip to represent each syllable and string them together. How many syllables does "bathtub" have? How about "sunflower"? How many three-syllable words can we think of? How many with four syllables?

Identifying New Words

Strategies used to identify new words are measured by questions 7, 8, 10, 11, 13, and 14 on the Reading Assessment.

When your child comes to an unknown word, he needs a number of good solid strategies to figure it out. Counting on one strategy, such as predicting what the word is or sounding the word out, is inefficient and will bog him down. Here are some ways to help your child expand his repertoire of strategies. You will quickly learn which question or response works best in any given situation.

HAVE FIVE MINUTES?

DO THESE ACTIVITIES WHILE READING WITH YOUR CHILD:

➤ Ask, "Which word would make sense here?" Remember, reading is the pursuit of meaning.

➤ Suggest that he skip the word, read on, and then come back to the word. Once your child has read on, he may be able to predict what the word is based on context. Some children like to replace the unknown word with "blank," on the first reading.

➤ Say, "Look at the first letters and last letters of the word." If a child is reading for meaning, he may need only the beginning and ending sounds to determine the word. This strategy is faster than sounding out an entire word.

➤ Ask, "Can you sound this word out?" (Do not ask this question if the word is not decodable. For instance, a child sounding out *"what"* would say *"wat."*) Read the tips on blending letters to sound out words, page 82, if you haven't done so already.

➤ Say, "See if the pictures can help you figure out that word." Looking for picture clues is an acceptable way to decode words when learning to read. Eventually, your child will be able to read without the support of illustrations, but he will apply these same skills when doing research.

➤ Provide the word if it is especially difficult and your child would otherwise become frustrated. Above all, you want to keep the reading as smooth and as pleasurable as possible. As your first grader reads, slip in the tougher words and keep up the momentum.

Once your child has begun to use a number of strategies, stop yourself from jumping in. If she mispronounces a word, remain silent. Again, remember that substitutions are normal. If she substitutes a word that does not make sense, it is better to give her time to correct herself. Let her know that all readers, even adult readers, come across words they don't know. And that sometimes we simply guess the meaning of the word and go on.

Reading Comprehension

Reading comprehension is measured by questions 9, 12, and 15 on the Reading Assessment.

How can we help our children understand what they read? For as long as anyone can remember, teachers have had children read passages and then answer a series of questions. These questions are intended to help children fully grasp the meaning of the text. But you must understand that comprehension does not occur *after* reading; it occurs *during* reading. Questions can help extend a child's understanding. But if your child is concentrating on each individual word on a page and not thinking about the meaning of the words, he will not be able to answer questions at the end.

It is therefore particularly important when children are beginning to read—focusing on letters and sounds and recalling words—that they also focus on meaning. Parents can play a vital role in ensuring that this happens by doing the following things, which will be discussed in detail:

1. Read to your child daily.
2. Help your child read with purpose.
3. Discuss the stories, and particularly the child's emotional reactions to the stories, as you are reading.
4. Reread favorite books.
5. Participate in activities that increase your child's vocabulary.
6. Encourage your child to read critically.
7. Extend the reading experience.

Reading to your child daily

This is the single most important thing you can do to help support your child's learning. By reading aloud, you provide her with an ear for book talk, a language that can be found only on the written page. Unless your child is an avid storyteller, it is unlikely that you would hear a sentence like this in her everyday speech: *"'Get down from there,' said the old woman as she chewed on a mangled piece of straw."* By reading to her, you introduce your first grader to the cadence of written language. This allows her to make predictions and to better understand what she reads on her own.

When reading aloud, you and your child explore the world of books together. She can ask you to clarify the meaning of a sentence or a word. She can say, "I don't get it. What's happening here?" When a child comes to expect meaning from a story, she will pursue it more avidly on her own.

Your first grader's listening skills are more advanced than her reading skills. Therefore, the stories you read aloud to her can be more complex— richer in language and meaning—than the stories she reads independently. By reading stories above her level, you give her the message that one day she'll be able to read them, too. Nothing motivates a child more than a desire to have access to really good stories.

Many parents read to their children at bedtime. This is an excellent time, but it certainly isn't the only time to read aloud. Have one family member read a mystery aloud on a long car ride. Read to your child in her fort, in the bath-tub, or in a tree house. Bring your favorite poem or an interesting article to the dinner table.

Here are some exceptional read-aloud selections that you and your child won't want to miss:

PICTURE BOOKS—FICTION
Alexander and the Terrible, Horrible, No Good, Very Bad Day, by Judith Viorst (Aladdin)
Beware of Boys, by Tony Blundell (Mulberry, Division of Morrow)
Bootsie Barker Bites, by Barbara Bottner (Putnam)

The Boy Who Swallowed Snakes, by Lawrence Yep (Scholastic)
The Iguana Brothers, by Tony Johnston (Scholastic)
Jamaica and Brianna, by Juanita Havill (Houghton Mifflin)
Kate's Giants, by Valiska Gregory (Candlewick)
King Bidgood's in the Bathtub, by Audrey Wood (Harcourt Brace)
Lilly's Purple Plastic Purse, by Kevin Henkes (Greenwillow)
Ma Dear's Aprons, by Patricia McKissack (Atheneum)
Martha Blah Blah, by Susan Meddaugh (Houghton Mifflin)
Merle & Jasper's Supper Caper, by Laura Rankin (Knopf)
Possum's Harvest Moon, by Anne Hunter (Houghton)
Ruby the Copycat, by Peggy Rathman (Scholastic)
Shy Vi, by Wendy Cheyette Lewison (Simon & Schuster)
Someplace to Go, by Maria Testa (Albert Whitman)
Something from Nothing, by Phoebe Gilman (Scholastic)
The Song of Mulan, by Jeanne M. Lee (Front Street)
The Story of Ferdinand, by Munro Leaf (Viking)
Where the Wild Things Are, by Maurice Sendak (Harper)

PICTURE BOOKS—NONFICTION
A Field Full of Horses, by Peter Hansard, and other nonfiction books in the
    Candlewick Read and Wonder series (Candlewick)
Bill Pickett: Rodeo Riding Cowboy, by Andrea D. Pinkney (Harcourt)
Eleanor, by Barbara Cooney (Viking) (the story of Eleanor Roosevelt)
The Extinct Alphabet Book, by Jerry Pallotta, and other alphabet books by
    this author focusing on the desert, the sea, insects, and more
    (Charlesbridge)
The Largest Dinosaurs, by Simon Seymour (Macmillan)
Learning to Swim in Swaziland, by Nila K. Leigh (Scholastic)
Nature! Wild and Wonderful, by Laurence Pringle (Richard C. Owens)
Pond Year, by Kathryn Lasky (Candlewick)
Space: A Three-Dimensional Journey, by Brian Jones (Dial)
When Birds Could Talk and Bats Could Sing, by Virginia Hamilton
    (Scholastic) (seven African-American trickster stories)
The Story of Ruby Bridges, by Robert Coles (Scholastic)

POETRY
All the Small Poems and Fourteen More, by Valerie Worth (Farrar, Straus &
    Giroux)
My Song Is Beautiful: Poems and Pictures in Many Voices, selected by Mary
    Ann Hoberman (Little, Brown)

Now We Are Six, by A. A. Milne (Dutton) (Don't miss this one! Your six-year-old will love the humor.)

Pass It On: African-American Poetry for Children, selected by Wade Hudson (Scholastic)

Talking Like the Rain: A Read-to-Me Book of Poems, edited by X. J. Kennedy, Dorothy Kennedy, and Jane Dyer (Little, Brown)

For a list of chapter books to read to your child, see Reading and Writing Enrichment, page 117.

Helping your child read with purpose

Learning to read can lead to many new and thrilling discoveries. For starters, a reader can: read a book or magazine for pleasure; find out how to send away for the toy on the back of the cereal box; learn more about a passionate interest such as eighteen-wheelers or dolphins; read a letter from a pen pal; surf the Internet; follow a map; and get help from an advice-for-children column.

When we read for a reason, like the ones listed above, we automatically read for meaning. Help your child develop a wide range of purposes for reading.

HAVE FIVE MINUTES?

➤Read to laugh out loud. First graders love riddles, jokes, and funny poetry. Read the more advanced books to your child, pausing to let him read the answers, the punch lines, or the final words, if they are predictable. Here are some very funny books to look for. Your child will want to read them again and again.

POETRY
Where the Sidewalk Ends; There's a Light in the Attic; and *Falling Up,* by Shel Silverstein (HarperCollins)

The New Kid on the Block; Something Big Has Been Here; and *A Pizza the Size of the Sun,* by Jack Prelutsky (Greenwillow)

The Funniest Poems: Poems That Make Kids Laugh, by Bruce Lansky (Meadowbrook Kids) (poems chosen by kids)

PICTURE BOOKS AND EASY-TO-READ BOOKS
Animals Should Definitely Not Wear Clothing, by Judi Barrett (Atheneum)

If You Give a Moose a Muffin and *If You Give a Mouse a Cookie,* by Laura Numeroff (HarperCollins)

George Shrinks, by William Joyce (HarperCollins, Scholastic)

Do Pirates Take Baths?, by Kathy Tucker (Whitman)

RIDDLE AND JOKE BOOKS

Spacey Riddles, by Katy Hall and Lisa Eisenberg (Puffin)

Knock-Knock Knees and Funny Bones, by Judith Mathews and Fay Robinson (Albert Whitman)

The Joke Book and *The Riddle Book,* by Roy McKie (Random House)

The Bailey School Kids Joke Book (Scholastic)

99 1/2 Gross Jokes, Riddles and Nonsense, by Holly Kowitt (Scholastic)

➤When your child asks, "What is a bush baby?" or "Do hurricanes only happen in the summer?" or "What's the smallest country in the world?" suggest that you find the answer together. You might look the subject up in an encyclopedia, do a search on the Internet, look at a globe, or visit the library to find out more.

Reference books can be enormously helpful in satisfying the curiosity of a first grader. You may not be able to invest in a brand-new encyclopedia at this time, but here are a few ways to build up a collection. Don't be discouraged if the collection is dated; much of the information remains the same and will serve your purposes:

- Buy a used encyclopedia from a library. Sometimes encyclopedias are sold at used-book sales, sometimes they are offered for sale at a silent auction at much less than the original price, and other times you simply need to let the librarian know that you are dying to own a used set.

- Search flea markets, used-book shops, yard sales, and your local want ads for children's visual encyclopedias, children's dictionaries, and other reference books.

- Reference books that you do want to be current, such as *The Guinness Book of World Records,* can be purchased inexpensively through school book clubs.

If you have the means and inclination to buy a few new reference books, here are some exceptional ones that are well worth the investment:

- *The Kingfisher First Encyclopedia* (Kingfisher, 1996). A beautifully illustrated volume introducing a wide range of topics. Each entry such as "Antarctica," "computers," "insects," or "sports" is given at least one full page of coverage with easy-to-understand text.

- *My First Book of Questions: Easy Answers to Hard Questions Children Ask* (Scholastic, 1992). Here are all those answers to kids' toughest questions (one question for each letter of the alphabet): What makes leaves change colors? Why does gravity make things fall down? Why are people different colors? You won't be able to put this book down.

- *My First Dictionary*, by Betty Root (Dorling Kindersley, 1993). Every word is illustrated in this beginning dictionary. It includes a number of dictionary games for skill development.

➤You can't imagine how influential it is for your child to see you choose reading over other activities. While you are reading, laugh out loud, share an interesting story or fact, and tell your child, "I can't do that right now. I'm at a really exciting part of my book."

HAVE MORE TIME?

➤Read to follow directions. Help your child use written directions to prepare food from a recipe, make a craft, plant an indoor garden, or order a toy from the back of the cereal box. There are many, many how-to books for children at your local library. Search for a new project to do together.

➤Expand your child's interests. If your child has a particular interest such as model cars, dinosaurs, soccer, rocks, or historical dolls, help her pursue those interests. Read information in books, in magazines, and on the Internet. Write letters to experts or stars. Suggest that your first grader keep a scrapbook of all the facts, interesting articles, and letters she's collected.

Discussing stories with your child

Perhaps you've tried to read to your first grader, and he's interrupted constantly. You read the first sentence. He wants to discuss the picture on the cover. You read the second sentence. He asks a question. You read the third sentence and he tells you about another book that this story reminds him of. Finally you sigh loudly and say, "Do you want to hear this story or not?"

As exasperating as these interruptions might be, your child is showing desirable reading behavior. By looking at the illustration on the cover, he's beginning to build up background knowledge that will provide hooks for the new information to hang on. Suppose that your child sees a picture of a cricket on the book cover and says, "I know what a cricket is. It's a bug. I've heard them chirp in the summer." This tells you he's halfway to understanding a book about a cricket who couldn't make a sound. If your child lives in the city and has never seen or heard a cricket, you can introduce this information while looking at the cover of the book.

Children frequently ask questions when a story is just beginning. They do this because they are trying to set the scene—create a mental picture. It's been discovered that children who have difficulty with reading often fail to visualize the story as they read. Where does the story take place? Who is there? What is the problem? These questions are answered in the opening paragraphs and are crucial to comprehending the story.

Discussing the story as you go along helps your child to process what has happened and to predict what will happen next. Whether your child is reading to you or you're reading to your child, discussions should be spontaneous—a voicing of interests or questions that naturally arise. If you try too hard to create discussion, especially by asking very specific questions such as "What did the bumblebee say to the cricket?" the reading will be too chopped up and boring and will ultimately become frustrating for both of you. Remember, your purpose is to explore books, not to test your child. So keep things light and enjoy the insights your budding reader shares.

HAVE FIVE MINUTES?

➤ Take time to study the illustrations before reading the story. Your child might mention the details she notices; predict what the book is going to be about; discuss whether she thinks the story will be funny, scary, or sad; make references to her own life and knowledge; or even recognize the name of the illustrator and mention other books he's done.

➤ Talk about story elements. "What's the main character like?" (character). "Where do you think this story takes place? When did this story happen? How can you tell?" (setting). "What problem does the main character have to solve?" (plot). "How do you think she'll solve this problem? How would you solve the problem if you were the hero?"

➤ Read a chapter book to your child and help him form mental images. Ask, "How do you picture the main character? What do you think this place looks like? How did you imagine the character doing that?" And then the most important follow-up question: "Why do you think so?"

➤ Discuss your child's emotional reactions to what is happening in the story. These links between feelings and information are wonderful learning opportunities.

➤ While reading together, give your child practice in drawing conclusions: How did Pooh know that the bees were suspicious? How do you know that Pipi isn't like other children? How do you think Curious George was feeling? Why?

➤ Have book talks at the dinner table. These talks can occur occasionally if you simply ask, "Did anyone read a good book today?" Or you could plan special nights in which each family member comes prepared to tell about a book.

HAVE MORE TIME?

➤ Plan a dinnertime book talk and suggest that each person come dressed as his or her favorite book character.

Rereading favorite books

Remember when your child was younger and he requested that you read the same book to him night after night? Well, he knew what was good for him. You may have tired of reading Margaret Wise Brown's *The Runaway Bunny*, but he was increasing his vocabulary, deepening his understanding, raising new questions, and learning the language of books.

Our minds tend to focus on one or two strands of learning at a time. So while you watch a movie for the first time, you probably focus on the drama and the story line. While watching it for the second time, you notice the details that create a realistic, funny, or frightening story and the clues that foreshadow what's to come. Perhaps during the third viewing, you recognize the themes of the movie and how they pertain to your life at this time. Or perhaps you just laugh harder because this time around you catch more of the humor.

Children gain as much by reading or hearing their favorite books again and again. While reading a range of new books your child acquires a *breadth* of information, while reading old familiars your child acquires a *depth* of information. Both are important.

HAVE FIVE MINUTES?

➤ Encourage your child to reread to you a book he's had success with.

➤ If your child regularly brings books home from school, ask that he choose a favorite and read it again. If your child particularly enjoyed a library book, renew it for another two weeks.

➤ Set aside one of the bookshelves in your home for "Favorite Books." Choose books from the shelf often.

➤ Keep all of your children's magazines. You'll be amazed at how many times your child returns to read them again and again.

HAVE MORE TIME?

➤ Reread a favorite chapter book. Marvel at the things that you and your child do not remember from your last reading.

Activities that increase your child's vocabulary

The more words your child knows, the more she will comprehend while reading.

HAVE FIVE MINUTES?

➤ Talk to your child often, and use complete sentences. Do not shy away from words that you fear your child will not understand. He will begin to comprehend their meaning within the context of what you are saying. Take the time to discuss a word when he says, "What does that mean?"

➤ Have your child listen to story tapes at home and in the car. Listening to stories is one of the best ways to increase a person's vocabulary. Most libraries include children's books on tape.

Music and accompanying songbooks are also a good choice for increasing your child's vocabulary. Two recommended selections are *When the Spirit Says Sing: A Read-Along, Sing-Along Coloring Book* (book and cassette) by Sandy Patton; and *Woody's 20 Grow Big Songs* by Woody Guthrie, HarperCollins (recording available).

➤ Whenever you go places, help your child notice and label the world around him. At the supermarket, introduce the words *butcher, deli-catessen, produce,* and *dairy products*. Better yet, see if your child can have brief glimpse of what goes on behind the scenes. Many of the chain supermarkets are happy to show children the large walk-in freezers and the deep ovens. When you go to the library, introduce the words *card catalog, nonfiction, fiction, periodicals,* and *circulation*. It's amazing how often we pass through these places without taking the time to share the language.

➤ Play quick word games. One easy game that you can play anywhere is Categories. One player chooses a category such as birds. Then you take turns naming as many birds as you can think of. The player who thinks of the last entry gets to pick the next category.

➤ Encourage your child to play imaginative games that involve talking. By playacting house, school, storekeeper, or vet, a child can practice using specific words. Provide dress-up clothes and props. Enacting adventures with action figures or stuffed animals can be equally useful. From time to time, introduce and participate in a new adventure. For instance, when a beloved toy monster was missing from one first grader's bed, it was quickly decided that this special friend was off on a jaunt through the solar system. Each night the family discussed where the monster was and what he was seeing. Before the little guy returned home (with the laundered sheets), the first grader had learned the names of all the planets, what they were like, and where they were located in the solar system.

➤If your child has difficulty with prepositions such as *beside, under, above, between,* here is a fun game to help reinforce her understanding of them. Open a large book and stand it on a table. The book will act as a screen. Now place a number of objects on the table, making sure that there are two of each. As you arrange half of the objects on your side of the screen, give your first grader directions so she can duplicate the arrangement. Say, for example, "Place the green block under the blue Lego. Place the yellow marble on the blue Lego." Remove the screen and see if the arrangements match.

HAVE MORE TIME?

➤Read a wide range of materials to your child and talk about what you read. Take home or subscribe to children's magazines or browse adult magazines such as *National Geographic* together. Here is a list of exceptional children's magazines:
  • *Chickadee*
    Young Naturalist Foundation
    Box 11314
    Des Moines, IA 50340
      Presents topics on science and nature in an entertaining way.
  • *Crayola Kids Magazine*
    1912 Grand Avenue
    Des Moines, IA 50309-3379
      Reprints a children's book in its entirety and presents crafts, puzzles, and activities that relate to a bimonthly theme.
  • *Highlights*
    803 Church Street
    Honesdale, PA 18431-1824
      You probably remember this magazine from the dentist's office you visited as a child. Although it does not have the slick appearance of newer magazines, it publishes quality stories. Many of the regular features such as Hidden Pictures, Goofus and Gallant, and the rebus stories are incredibly popular with six- and seven-year-olds.

- *Kid City*
  Children's Television Workshop
  Box 53349
  Boulder, CO 80322
    Lively, amusing articles on a range of topics for children six to ten years of age.
- *Ranger Rick*
  National Wildlife Federation
  1400 16th Street, NW
  Washington, DC 20036
    Exceptional photographs accompany articles that relate to nature, conservation, the outdoors, and natural science.
- *Spider*
  315 Fifth Street
  Peru, IL 61354
    Quality literature and activities with high kid-appeal.

➤ Create stories together. Take turns telling stories, or build a single story in which you take turns adding parts.

➤ Have your child make puppets and then use the puppets to tell or retell stories. One of the simplest ways to make puppets is to draw a character on paper, cut the character out, and use glue to mount the character on the end of a Popsicle or craft stick.

➤ Take your child to museums, concerts, and plays. Afterward, discuss what you see and hear.

➤ Read children's classics to your child. Many of the classics are written with a cadence and words that are seldom heard in today's world. But this does not make them irrelevant. On the contrary, these books will help your child develop an ear for new words. Eventually we all learn that we can determine a word's meaning from listening to the context—the words around it. Listening to timeless literature such as Thorton Burgess's *Old Mother West Wind Stories* or traditional stories such as Brer Rabbit, children stretch their understanding of language as well as their imaginations. You'll also find it fun to revisit the stories you read as a child.

➤ Choose a topic for you and your child to study in depth. Search for information from a variety of sources. For instance, if you decide to build a birdhouse, you'll need to learn about birds. You could read books and field guides, visit the local Audubon Society, talk to a local expert or to someone on the Internet. Then of course you would need to purchase the right materials and tools, which might take you an on another interesting course.

➤ Play Junior Pictionary by Parker Brothers. Children take turns reading a card and drawing a picture while other players guess the word being drawn.

Encouraging your child to read critically

You can help your first grader use higher-level thinking skills to apply knowledge to his own life, to analyze information and draw conclusions, to synthesize old and new knowledge, and to evaluate what he reads.

HAVE FIVE MINUTES?

➤ Discuss advertising on cereal boxes, newspaper ads, billboards, and television. What is real? What is fantasy?

➤ Read picture book or beginning biographies with your child. (Your librarian will direct you to some exceptional life stories for young children.) Ask your child to make comparisons. Are you and this person similar in any way? In what ways are you different? Do you think this person made good decisions? Why or why not?

➤ After reading a story together, ask one of these provocative questions:
  • What was the problem in this story? Can you think of another way the problem could have been solved?
  • What was your favorite part of this story? Why? What was your least favorite part? Why?
  • Which character in the story would you like to be? Why?
  • Did you like the ending? Why or why not? Can you make up a new ending to the story?
  • Does this book remind you of any other books? In what ways?
  • Do you think this is a good book? Why or why not?

➤ Choose a bookshelf for the books your child likes best. Let your child be the judge and choose the books that merit a place on this shelf.

➤ Read the car ads in the newspaper. Then invite your child to design a totally new car and to write an ad to sell it.

HAVE MORE TIME?

➤ Read a story together. Then you and your first grader, separately, write down your reactions to the book. (It's okay if only your first grader can read his response.) Then take turns reading aloud what you wrote.

Extending the reading experience

If your child is interested, suggest he do a project related to a book he's read. This is a good alternative to watching TV or playing video games, and it helps reinforce the notion that your family values books.

HAVE FIVE MINUTES?

➤ Have your child act out a favorite scene from the book. (Beware: first graders love to plan. Instead of acting out a scene, your child may choose to do a full-scale production. If so, set a future time for the performance.)

➤ Have your child draw a picture to illustrate a book that has no (or few) illustrations. This will help him develop his powers of mental imagery—a required skill for reading comprehension.

➤ First graders love maps. If appropriate, suggest your child draw an illustrated map of the route the main character took in the story.

HAVE MORE TIME?

➤ Invite your child to make a construction inspired by the story. For instance, a child who reads *The Little Mouse, the Red Ripe Strawberry, and the Big Hungry Bear*, by Don and Audrey Wood, might make a bear trap. A child who reads *A House Is a House for Me*, by Mary Ann Hoberman, might make the perfect house for an imaginary creature. Constructions can be made from recyclable materials such as empty cartons, toilet paper tubes, craft sticks, or heavy paper. Use your imagination and whatever you have available.

➤ Why not help your child prepare a meal that the main character in the story is sure to love? What might you and he concoct after reading *Blueberries for Sal* or *Stone Soup*? Have your first grader explain to family members and guests why he chose this menu.

➤ Videotape your child performing the part of the main character. When your child retells a story, he gains practice in recalling story events in sequence. He also gains more knowledge of story structure as he struggles to solve that character's problem. And you, the camera person, will certainly be presented with a dramatic treat!

➤ Help your child find other books by a favorite author or illustrator. You might suggest that your child write to the author or illustrator and send the letter along to the publisher. Many authors are diligent about writing back. If you have Internet access you may want to see if the author has a Web page, in which case you could reach him or her by E-mail.

➤ If your child enjoys nonfiction, take her someplace where she can find out more about the subject.

Reading Fluency

Reading fluency is measured by question 16 on the assessment.

First grade teachers often talk of the reading click. One day a child reads a simple story laboriously, pounding out each word. The next day she picks up a book and reads more quickly, more effortlessly, more fluently. It's as if the brain has carved new pathways. Suddenly all the necessary connections are made simultaneously.

We can't rush the brain's word processing system, but there are a few simple ways that parents can guide their child toward more natural, fluent reading. Try these.

HAVE FIVE MINUTES?

➤ First graders often use their fingers to mark their place while they read. Provide your child with a bookmark instead. Placing a bookmark along the bottom of a line of text will help your child move vertically down the page. It will also encourage her to scan with her eyes rather than reading the text word for word.

➤ Some children benefit from echo reading. Next time your child is reading a book at her level, read aloud right along with her, providing the correct pacing and voice intonation. Read the book twice to give your child a feeling of accomplishment.

➤ Encourage risk-taking. Your child may be trying too hard for perfection. Let her know that all readers, even grown-ups, misread words. Explain that when a word doesn't make sense, readers simply go back and try the sentence again. Continue reading aloud to your child often. Point out the times that you stumble over words or correct yourself.

➤ If your child insists on sounding out every word, she's probably relying too heavily on this strategy. When she comes to a word she doesn't know, ask: "What would make sense here?" or have her skip the word and read on. She can come back and reread the sentence, supplying the word from the context.

➤ Make sure that your child is not choosing books that are too difficult. You want your child to experience the success of reading fluently, and to build upon this success. Teachers often suggest that children use a five finger check to determine whether a book is too hard. Have your child put a finger in the air every time she comes to a word she doesn't know. If she puts five fingers in the air on a single page, the book is too difficult.

There are many beginning reader series for children. Here is a list of some of the most popular titles, including picture books that can be read by budding readers.

BOOKS FOR BEGINNING READERS

Frog and Toad, Frog and Toad are Friends, Mouse Tales, and more, by Arnold Lobel (HarperCollins)

Itchy Itchy Chicken Pox, My Tooth Is About to Fall Out, Pizza Party, Soccer Game, First Grade Friends, The Sword in the Stone, by Grace Maccarone (Scholastic)

George and Martha Rise and Shine, by James Marshall (Houghton Mifflin) (Marshall's other books are not as easy to read as this title)

There's an Alligator Under My Bed, Dial; *What Do You Do With a Kangaroo?* and the Little Critter books, by Mercer Mayer (Scholastic)

Gus and Grandpa, Gus and Grandpa Ride the Train, and more by Claudia Mills (Farrar, Straus & Giroux)

A Kiss for Little Bear, Little Bear's Friend, and three other Little Bear books, by Else Holmelund Minarik (HarperCollins)

Henry and Mudge: The First Book, Henry and Mudge in Puddle Trouble, and many more, by Cynthia Rylant (Simon & Schuster). Also see the Mr. Putter and Tabby series (Harcourt Brace).

One Fish, Two Fish, Red Fish Blue Fish, The Cat in the Hat, The Foot Book, Hop on Pop, and many more, by Dr. Seuss (Random House)

COLLECTIONS OF EASY-TO-READ STORIES:

Ready . . . Set . . . Read, compiled by Joanna Cole and Stephanie Calmenson (Doubleday). This book contains some of the best stories by Lobel, Seuss, Maurice Sendak, and more. See also *Bug in a Rug,* by Cole and Calmenson.

Night House Bright House, by Monica Wellington (Dutton) (Rebus rhymes about different rooms in a house)

PICTURE BOOKS

These wonderful picture books are a little more difficult than predictable books (page 76), but they're still easy to read:

Any Kind of Dog, by Lynn Reisser (Greenwillow)

Contrary Mary and Daisy Dare, by Anita Jeram (Candlewick)

Dear Mr. Blueberry, by Simon James (Simon & Schuster) (Letters between a child and a teacher)

How to Lose All Your Friends, by Nancy Carlson (Puffin)

My Best Friend, by Pat Hutchins (Greenwillow)

No One Told the Aardvark, by Deborah Eaton and Susan Halter (Charlesbridge)

On a Hot, Hot Day, by Nicki Weiss (Putnam)

The Pig in the Pond, by Martin Waddell (Candlewick.)

Rain Talk, by Mary Serfozo (Margaret K. McElderry Books)

Tick-Tock, by Eileen Browne (Candlewick)

Toby, Where Are You?, by William Steig (HarperCollins)

The Train to Lulu's, by Elizabeth Fitzgerald Howard (Aladdin)

Writing Stages and Exercises

You will need one or more writing samples, as suggested in the Writing Assessment, to determine your child's current stage of writing development.

Learning to write is part of the process of learning to communicate—a process that is not unlike the process of learning to talk. This process is constantly evolving. From the very moment when your child picked up a pencil and scribbled on a sheet of paper (or a wall), he was a writer. First a child scribbles. Then he makes scratches that become closer and closer approximations to letters. Once your child becomes familiar with the sounds of letters, he carefully chooses appropriate letters to make words. The words themselves evolve until they approximate standard spelling. The child strings words together into sentences and sentences into paragraphs. And at every step of the process, he is communicating a message. He is thinking about what he wants to say and how he wants to say it.

This chapter will help you discover where your child is in this process. You may find that he does not fit into a single clear-cut stage. Children seldom do. Instead, they waver between stages, one day remembering to include a vowel in each word, the next day leaving the vowel out. But these pages will give you a road map of sorts and many ideas for helping your child take the next turn.

It should be said, however, that although these ideas are helpful, you have probably begun doing the single most important thing you can do to help your child flourish as a writer—by being a good audience.

Every writer, no matter what the age, needs a good listener. An audience that listens to a piece of writing and responds appropriately with an "Ooh" or an "I remember that!" or with a laugh. Here are a few more tips for responding to your child appropriately:

- Try to respond to the *meaning* or the freshness of a written piece first and foremost. Imagine writing a story about an event that is important to you, only to have the first person you show it to tell you that you spelled a word wrong or that you left out a period. Instead of looking at the mechanics of the writing, tell your child how the writing makes you feel, what it reminds you of, or what you especially liked—even if the writing is only one word.

- Be specific when pointing out what your child has done well. Rather than saying "This is very good," you might say "You gave so many details about the party that I really felt as if I was there." Or "Wow! I see the sun and you wrote the word 'sun.' You heard the letters *s* and *n*." If you are specific about what is working, he'll be able to repeat his success.

- To help your child extend his writing, ask questions: What did the mouse do next? How will the mouse solve this problem? How will your story end?

- What if you can't read your child's writing? Ask your first grader to read it to you. Then ask if you can write your own words on the page so both of you will always know what it says. If he agrees, record his words in small letters somewhere discreetly on the page. Make sure that he understands that his written words are more important than yours. You might point out that there are lots of written languages that you can't read, but you're learning to read kid language.

- When is it appropriate to focus on spelling and mechanics? After you have been a good audience. Then you might (not every time certainly) point out *one* thing that your child is on the verge of knowing. For instance, you might say, "Look! You remembered that the word 'saw' has an *s* and a *w*. That is very close to the dictionary spelling. I'll write the word 'saw' on a card for you so you can remember that 'saw' is spelled *s-a-w*."

Another way to help your child, no matter what stage he is in, is provide him with his own space to write. A small desk or table and an assortment of writing tools will keep your child motivated to write for all sorts of purposes. Here is a list of things you might provide for your young writer:

- pencils, markers, crayons, pens
- paper of all sorts and sizes, including adding machine tapes and large rolls of butcher paper

- a notebook
- stationery and envelopes
- ink stamps with his name and address or the date
- a stapler for making books
- glue sticks
- scissors

Writing, like most skills, is learned best by doing. So encourage your child to write often and for many reasons. And in the same way that you honored and reinforced your child's attempts to talk, enjoy and support your child's attempts to communicate by writing. The child who feels confident as a writer has been given a lifelong gift.

Stage 1: Beginning Literacy

Children in this stage know that writing and letters go together. They may write a string of random letters, usually without spaces, to convey a message or a story. In addition, they demonstrate their understanding that print should appear in lines and that longer messages have more letters. They may also write a few memorized words such as their own name or the names of family members.

If your child is in this stage, you'll want to praise him for his writing efforts and guide him toward matching consonants with word sounds. Children move from this stage to writing one consonant, sometimes two, to represent each

A tiger is swimming. Jacob

"This is cursive writing."

Katie (random letters) MOM

word. Your child will be most successful if you trust these stages and do not seam eager to rush the writing process.

Chances are, you've already discovered the letter sound activities in Letter Sounds, page 66. You'll want to explore or revisit some of those activities as well as the ones listed here.

HAVE FIVE MINUTES?

➤ Reread a favorite story to your child. As you read, point to each word. This will give him more information about how print works.

➤ Many children at this stage draw as a means of communicating. Their story is told in pictures. After your child has drawn a picture, say, "Tell me about your picture." Then suggest that your child write one word to go with the illustration. Ask, "What word would you like to write?" Then "What sounds do you hear in that word?" Stretch the word out so your child can hear the sounds. For instance, if the word is rocket, say "r—o—c—k—e—t." When your child isolates a sound, help him to match the sound to the appropriate letter and write it on the paper. Do not expect your child to hear *all* of the sounds in the word. If he hears only one or two sounds, be pleased for him.

➤ When reading a book together, ask your child, "What do you know about the print on this page?" Your child might point to the letter his name begins with or to other letters he recognizes. If so, ask him, "Do you know what sound that letter makes?" Brainstorm other words that have the same beginning sound. Teach him the letters sounds in this way, but introduce only a couple of new sounds at a time.

➤ Make a list, such as a grocery list or a list of things to do together. Have your child write the first letter for every word. Then you can complete the words.

➤ While your child is involved in dramatic playing, help him make labels. Label buildings made of blocks: garage, hospital, fire station. Label animal habitats: forest, mountains, river. Label parts of a house: kitchen, bedroom, workshop. Each time your child writes a label, have him record the sounds he hears.

➤ Children at this stage need help recalling the different letters. Tape an alphabet chart on the desk, table, or counter where he writes. You can purchase a small alphabet chart at teacher supply stores or photocopy the one provided in the back of this book on page 189. Your child may not have enough eye-hand coordination to use a wall chart yet, so you may want to ask the teacher if he can attach a similar chart to his desk at school.

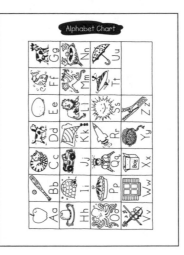

➤ Be willing to take dictation. Many children are pleased to have their oral stories recorded by an adult. Taking dictation helps children structure their thoughts and develop a written voice. By looking at what you've recorded, your first grader can see how words and sentences are formed. You might want to use discretion, however. Some educators feel that if you get into the habit of recording all of your child's words, he will not get the practice he needs to grow into a confident writer.

➤ Suggest that your child make a field manual of your yard, a park, or even his bedroom. Staple paper together to make a book. On each page have your child draw one object from the chosen environment. Suggest that he write one word on each page so others will know what to look for when they visit this special place.

➤ If your child is having difficulty forming letters, you may want to work together on art or sewing projects to help strengthen those small muscles and develop eye-hand coordination. Your library will have many books with craft suggestions. Choose projects that you and your child will enjoy working on together.

Stage 2: Identifying Consonants

Children in this stage begin by writing one consonant—usually the beginning sound—to represent each word. Then they move to writing initial and final consonant sounds. Children may not leave spaces between words yet, or they may use dots or dashes to represent the spaces. This is perfectly acceptable strategy, and the child will stop using it within a short time. Some sight words and frequently used words, such as "and" and "me," may be correctly spelled.

Many children will choose consonants because of the name of the letter, rather than the sound of the letter. Say the name of this letter: y. Now say these words: *why, went, where*. The beginning of these words sound a lot more like *y* than "double-u." Other frequent substitutions are *h* for *ch* and *r* for vowel sounds.

helicopter	*Dear Santa, I want a Polly Pocket and a Troll Kit and some Barbie clothes.*

If your child is in this stage, you'll want to help her in several ways:
- Continue writing the sounds she hears.
- Help her identify the sounds of letters rather than their names.
- Use an increasing number of sight words.
- Develop an awareness of vowels in words.

HAVE FIVE MINUTES?

➤ Set up mailboxes for you and your child. Exchange letters frequently. Try to use some of the same words your child uses so she can see the correct spelling.

➤ Suggest your child "spy" on your pet, shoppers in the grocery store, or people who pass by your home. Have her record everything she sees. Don't worry about correct spelling. The idea is to have your child write, write, write. The more she writes, the more she'll want to know about writing.

➤ First graders love subversive rhymes and wordplay. Chances are your child has already learned a number of ditties that have been passed along orally for generations. Perhaps she's learned "Row, row, row your boat gently down the stream. Throw your teacher overboard and listen to her scream." Or "I see London, I see France . . ." You get the idea. Have your child keep a journal of her favorite ones. You'll be surprised by how much she can write with the right kind of motivation!

➤ There are many situations in which you can tell your child to put something in writing: You don't like peas for dinner? Put your reasons in writing and I'll consider serving a different vegetable. Want a later bedtime? Put your reasons in writing and I'll consider letting you stay up a little later. Do consider making the changes whenever possible, and announce your decision in a note to your child.

➤ Study your child's writing. Does she consistently choose consonants because of the letter name rather than the sound the letter makes? If so, reteach those letter sounds using some of the activities on pages 66–70.

➤ Write the five vowels, *a, e, i, o,* and *u* on a card for your child. Explain that every word in the English language has one of these vowels. When reading, challenge your child to find a word that doesn't have a vowel. If she finds a word such as *"cry"* or *"dry,"* explain that tricky *y* can sometimes be a vowel. Praise her for the discovery and add *y* to her card.

➤ Choose a picture book with just a few sentences on each page, and read it to your child. Ask your first grader, "Which word on this page has the most vowels? Can you find a word on another page that has more vowels?"

HAVE MORE TIME?

➤ Nothing empowers a first grade writer like making a book. Staple sheets of paper inside a construction paper cover, or use dental floss to stitch a book together. (Dental floss is strong and easy to pull through paper.) Then invite your child to record anything she wishes. In addition to stories or diary entries your child might write:
  • An autobiography beginning with her birth or earliest memory
  • A joke book
  • A nonfiction book about a special interest
  • Poems (if you've read poetry to your child she'll have no problem writing a few of her own.)
  • A book of favorite words
  • A travel log
  • Captions for a book of photo memories.

Stage 3: Transitional Spelling

At this stage, children are writing words with both consonants and vowels (although early on, the vowel might serve only as a marker, and the child might use any vowel at all). The writing will still contain a good deal of practice spelling, but children can now apply their knowledge of sound combinations (*sh, oo, ch*) and standard spelling patterns (*ing*, silent *e*). With regular writing practice, the child will incorporate an increasing number of sight words and standard spellings.

At the transitional stage of writing, children should also be able to write five or more sentences about a topic, use punctuation at the end of a sentence, and capitalize the first word of a sentence, the pronoun "I," and proper nouns.

The task for the child at this stage is to continue working on all of these skills while giving more attention to the purpose, organization, and creativity of writing projects. This sounds like a tall order, but it need not be. If children are given a multitude of natural and meaningful writing goals (writing an invitation to a slumber party), rather than trite or contrived exercises (five sen-

"Time for bed, Tommy," said Tommy's mom. "I don't want to go to bed!" said Tommy. He hid behind the couch.

tences telling what you would do if you were a worm on a hook), they will develop an interest in writing and an understanding of why we need to write well.

It is difficult for any writer, but especially for a child in the transitional stage, to focus simultaneously on the mechanics of writing (penmanship, spelling, punctuation) and the writing content (creativity, sequence, presentation of information). It is therefore best to suggest that your child write a draft first. While writing a rough draft, he can add words, cross them out, record misspelled words, all without interrupting his drive to communicate effectively. Once he has successfully recorded his thoughts and revised his sentences, he can edit his work to correct mechanical errors.

HAVE FIVE MINUTES?

➤ As your child begins to write for a broader audience, he'll become increasingly aware of the need for standard writing conventions. For example, if his friends are to be able to read an invitation to a party, he will need to spell the words correctly. And if his friends are to make sense of the message, he must use punctuation and capital letters. Here are a few suggestions for helping your child write for a larger audience:

- Thank-you notes
- Invitations
- Letters to relatives, pen pals, authors, or editors of magazines
- Cards for special occasions
- Signs to be posted on a door or on a lemonade stand
- Stories to be submitted for publication (magazines that publish children's writing are listed on pages 119–20).
- Notes for a bulletin board
- A self-published newspaper
- Games to be played by friends and family members
- A scrapbook with special notes, cards, photographs, and ticket stubs (Have your first grader write a sentence or two to accompany each memento. Explain that he'll want to look back on the scrapbook as he gets older.)
- Bumper stickers

➤ Words can be found in books, on packages, on messages on many a refrigerator, and on maps. Encourage your child to use these sources to find the correct spelling.

➤ Provide your child with a good picture dictionary. Learning to spell is a combination of analyzing the sounds of a word *and* visual memory. Many children will happily read a pictorial dictionary as well as use it to check spellings. Most of these dictionaries are set up so children can find words in ways other than alphabetical order. For instance, *Writing Sight Words* by Heather Amery (Usborne) provides a thousand words separated by category such as kitchen words and school words.

➤ When reading a romping tale aloud, have your child make a noise to represent each end punctuation. For instance, he could clap on a period, say "Mmm?" for a question mark, and clack his tongue or pop his finger against his cheek for an exclamation point. Don't be surprised if he repeats the noises while writing his own story!

HAVE MORE TIME?

➤ Does your child have a special interest? Birds? Baseball? Music? If so, you might want to make an *A* to *Z* word chart to use as a reference. Take a large sheet of butcher paper and divide it into fourteen squares. Write two letters in the corner of each square (popular *t* and *s* can have their own squares). Then have your child brainstorm all the words she knows that are related to her interest. Write each word, spelled correctly, in the appropriate square. Now when she writes about her passion, she can look up the correct spelling.

Writing Roadblocks

Some children seem to have great difficulty writing even a few words. They may write the same words over and over, using little imagination or original expression. What causes these blocks to creative writing?

Some children lack small motor control, and for them, writing is torture. They should be allowed to use computers or to give dictation. Certain other children have a condition that prevents them from making writing connections. They probably began writing with enthusiasm but are not making progress at the same pace as their classmates. If your child's reading and writing skills are not progressing at a normal rate, perhaps her teacher can arrange for appropriate testing and support services.

However, if she seems to be progressing in reading and skills but draws pictures for most of a writing period, or writes the same words or sentences every day, or often says, "I hate to write!" then her problem may be due to a fear of taking risks.

We associate risk-taking with athletics or riding a roller coaster rather than with learning. In truth, however, all learning, and particularly writing, requires a good amount of risk-taking. Think of the challenges! Or, instead, think of the messages a child risks hearing:

I can't read what you wrote.
That's not how the word is spelled!
That's not how it happened.
You left out the part about . . .
Why don't you write about real [imaginary, funny, serious] things.
How come you always write about dinosaurs?
Haven't you learned about periods and capital letters?
This is silly.
You can do better than this.

And even in the absence of criticism, some children (like many adults) are simply afraid to tackle the blank page. They may be thinking,

So much happened. It would take me all day to tell it all.
I don't know how to spell those words.
Everybody else has such good ideas; mine would be stupid.
My teacher said she liked my story about dinosaurs, I'll keep writing about dinosaurs.
I don't know how to begin.

Fortunately there are many ways that a parent can support and encourage risk-taking. And when your first grader takes a chance and succeeds, that feeling of success will spur him on more.

HAVE FIVE MINUTES?

➤ Be a cheerleader. Whenever your child records words, let him know, by mentioning what you see, how proud you are: "You used letters to label this drawing! Here is a fire truck and you heard the letter *f!*" "You wrote a list. Now, that was a clever way to keep track of your collection!" "You described our trip well. I feel as if I'm there all over again!"

➤ In some classrooms, children are asked to move too quickly away from drawing to writing words only. For many first graders who need to draw as a form of prewriting (prewriting is generating and organizing thoughts, discovering what one wants and needs to say), this is counterproductive. If you think this may be the case, suggest that your child do a good deal of drawing at home. Then help him find a story in his drawing. After he has stated his ideas orally, say, "Tomorrow you can write about this story in school."

➤ Have your child draw a picture. Say, "Tell me about your picture." And then say, "If you were going to write those words, where would you put them on the page?" Have your child point to the place. You may be amazed at how this simple three-step exercise gets your first grader going in the right direction.

➤ If writing his own story seems too overwhelming, have him pattern a story after a favorite storybook or song. For instance, he could rewrite the song "Old McDonald," but instead of a farm, Old McDonald could have a ball team, a restaurant, or a school. Your child can change the words to make a lively rendition.

➤ Have your child write a story to accompany a page in a wordless picture book.

➤ Buy a set of magnet words for children at a bookstore. Place the words on your refrigerator and invite your whole family to write with them. Writing with magnetic words helps children to see that words can be moved, substituted, rearranged. Writing is not something he needs to do perfectly.

➤ Write a story as a family. When everyone gets into the act, the awful burden of having to begin, or of being the sole author, is lifted.

➤ Have your child keep a journal for a favorite stuffed animal, action fig-ure, or doll. Periodically, your child can tell about the amazing happen-ings in the life of his pretend friend. For some reason, children are more comfortable writing the adventures of a beloved toy than writing about their own thoughts and feelings.

➤ What is your child's area of expertise? Does he know the name of every NBA basketball team? Can he make the best peanut butter and banana sandwich you've ever tasted? Help him to see that he has skills to teach others. Have him write a book of instructions about his interests.

HAVE MORE TIME?

➤ Create a dialogue letter with your child. Begin by asking a question such as *"What would you like to do today?"* Have your child respond in writing. Then ask another related question. Keep the letter going for as long as you both remain interested.

➤ Cut out magazine pictures of settings. Ask your child to imagine what could happen in that setting. If your child loves to play with paper dolls, cut out pictures of people for her to manipulate in the settings. Then sug-gest that she write about what happened.

➤ Buy the book *Free Stuff for Kids,* published by Meadowbrook. This book lists hundreds of places kids can write to receive "safe, fun and informa-tive things."

➤ Write messages and put them in your child's lunch box. He can then write messages for yours.

Reading and Writing Enrichment

The range of reading and writing abilities in a first grade classroom is tremendous. At any time you could walk in and see one child reading a little book with two words on each page, another child reading Doctor Seuss's *Hop on Pop*, a third child discovering the delight of chapter books, and yet another reading a novel on a fourth grade level. In the writing corner, one child might be drawing pictures with one-word captions while another child is writing a sequel to a favorite movie.

If your child is operating at the upper end of this range, you will want to ensure that he is being supported, in school and out, as a continually growing reader and writer. Some teachers have been known to dismiss the particular needs of a talented student with the message, "We don't need to be concerned about his language arts skills. Let's talk about other areas." This attitude is neither justifiable nor fair. Every child in the classroom is entitled to the following:

- The opportunity to read books of genuine interest on the appropriate grade level. If you find that your child does not have access to books at his level, or time to read them, make an appointment to talk with his teacher. Together you can come up with a workable plan. If your child's classroom does not have many books at the upper range, offer to send them in with your child. Your town librarian can recommend some wonderful fiction and nonfiction titles. (There is a list of recommended books, new and old, at the end of this chapter.)

- Some time in which to choose his own writing topics, and the encouragement to occasionally approach a teacher's assignment in new and imaginative ways.
- The opportunity to discuss reading and writing with those who share the same interests and abilities. Reading and writing are social as well as intellectual experiences. "Have you come to the part when . . . ?" "Were you surprised that . . . ?" We need to share our enthusiasm for favorite endeavors. Some schools provide this experience with a program for gifted and talented students. Others allow first graders to work with children from other classrooms. A child might join a group or be paired with a reading or writing buddy from an upper grade. And in many schools, children can search the Internet for others who share the same interests and passion for reading and writing.

One word of caution. Although your child is a good reader, he is also a first grader. First graders love literature of all kinds. Just because a child can read a chapter book or a novel does not mean that he won't want to continue to read emergent readers (they're fun and silly) or picture books. Many picture books, in fact, are written at a higher level than chapter books. If a child is sent out of the room too often or doesn't get a chance to read zany big books with the rest of the class, he is likely to be discouraged from reading. Rejoice in your child's interest in all kinds of reading. Keep in mind that even though you are able to read literary works, you probably also love a fast read and even enjoy the comics now and then.

It is equally important that you keep reading aloud to your child. Some first graders actually have misgivings about learning to read. They fear that once they can read on their own, their parents will stop reading aloud to them. You can assure your child that this won't happen. By reading together, you will not only retain this lovely, intimate time but also help your child discover books that he wouldn't normally choose for himself. You will continue to introduce him to new vocabulary, ideas and concepts, and you will give him the chance to continue to emulate an efficient dramatic reader—you!

You and your first grader can vary the way in which you read together. Take turns being the reader. Borrow two copies of a book from the library and take turns reading the same story. Perhaps one of you can read the narration while the other reads the dialogue. One night your child can choose *Curious George;* the next night you can choose *The Wind in the Willows.*

Good reading and good writing are inextricably linked. Everything that your child reads will inform his writing style. Everything that he writes will expand his reading ability. Here are some activities that will challenge your child further:

➤ Have your child write a holiday wish list for a favorite story character. Taking that character's interests and concerns into consideration, what would he like most to receive?

➤ Talk in similes: "I'm as hungry as an elephant with a knot tied in his trunk," or "I'm as sleepy as an eagle without a nest." Invite your child to respond with his own imaginative similes.

➤ After reading a book that both you and your child enjoyed, play the "What if" game. For instance, after reading *Charlotte's Web,* by E. B. White, you could ask, "What if Templeton had saved Wilbur instead of Charlotte? What would he have done?" Or "What if Wilbur was more like Curious George? What would he have done differently?" Be aware, however, that this game can be quite difficult for some children who are just beginning to be able to infer and draw conclusions.

➤ Suggest that your child write a song or two. You may want to read *Sing, Sophie!* by Dayle Ann Dodds (Candlewick). In this story, Sophie composes her own country-western songs: "My dog ran off, my cat has fleas, my fish won't swim, and I hate peas." This funny book will inspire everyone to write their own lyrics.

➤ Does your child have a favorite book series? Suggest that he write his own sequel. (It will, in all likelihood, be a story rather than a 92-page book.)

➤ Next time you make a routine trip to the grocery store, have your child serve as your navigator. Ask him to tell you how to get there. If he doesn't tell you to turn in time, keep on going straight. Then have him give you the information to correct the route! This is a wonderful exercise to help build a child's awareness of audience, sequence, and detail. Your child will simply think it's fun that he's in control of the car!

➤ Is your child always looking for something to write about? Suggest that he keep an idea box. Have him store his favorite photographs in a shoe box, along with pictures from magazines, postcards, little toys that have meaning, favorite words cut out of junk mail or written on a card. Then when he wants to write about something new, have him draw two items from the box. How are these things related? What do they remind him of?

➤ Subscribe to magazines that publish writing by children. Encourage your child to submit a story or poem of his own. Here are the addresses:

- *Stone Soup*
Children's Art Foundation
Box 83
Santa Cruz, CA 95063
    Every issue is devoted to art and writing by children.
- *Highlights*
803 Church Street
Honesdale, PA 18431-1824
    Art and writing by children are published in each issue.
- *Kids at Home*
Box 363
Astoria, OR 97103
    A magazine written by and for home schoolers. Children can also submit stories by E-mail.

➤ Some magazines for adults are appropriate to read with your child. Many children are fascinated by *National Geographic* and *Outside* magazine. If you and your child share a special interest, find a trade magazine that you can pore over together.

➤ The computer is a wonderful learning tool for children at any stage of learning, but for the proficient reader and writer, the computer is a gateway to paradise. A number of excellent software programs (see the list of resources below) allow children to write and illustrate their own books. And the Internet offers dozens of sites for children to exchange book reviews and publish their own writing. Is your child interested in fantasy? Poetry? Use your search engine, type in "kid's writing" and choose the link that is best suited to your child's interest.

The following books review children's software. They can direct you to the most appropriate program for your child:
- *The Best Toys, Books, Videos and Software for Kids 1997: 1000+ Kid-tested Classic and New Products for Ages 0–10,* by Joanne Oppenheim
- *The Family PC Software Buyer's Guide,* by Kurt Carlson and Valle Dwight
- *Kidware: The Parent's Software Guide, vol. 1,* by Michael C. Perkins and Celia Nunez
- *Home Education Resource Guide,* by Cheryl Gordon

➤ When your child writes about a nonfiction topic ask, *"What is the main idea of your work?"* Help your child understand that nonfiction pieces have a main idea presented at the beginning, followed by details that support the main idea.

➤ Is your child capable but resistant to reading? (Some children at this age get hooked into book series and are often unwilling to try new literature.) If so, turn to the back cover or the inside flap of a new book and read it aloud to your child. Discuss what the book might be about. Often this is enough to pique your child's interest and break down the barriers that have kept him from wanting to try it.

HAVE MORE TIME?

➤ Suggest to your first grader that she create a board game that requires reading. She might design a trail for her game with instructions such as "Move ahead 3 spaces" or "Go back 1 space" in each square. Or she might make cards with instructions such as "Pat your nose" that players must follow when drawn. In addition to using her reading and writing skills, she'll also learn a good deal about math (addition, subtraction, probability, and logical thinking). Then have a ball playing the game with your child!

➤ Suggest to your child that she be the official record keeper for a series of events. For instance, she could keep records of the planting, weeding, growth, and harvesting of the garden. Or she could keep track of the meals that the family has eaten in the past week. Who liked them? Who didn't? Who has new suggestions for the shopper and cook? Honor this job your child has taken on. Be sure to ask for the information regularly.

➤ Perhaps a number of odd jobs need to be done around the house and you're willing to pay someone to do them. Give your first grader the details. Introduce her to the classified ads in your local newspaper so she can see how ads are written. Then have her write some help wanted ads. She can then post the classified ads where everyone can read them. Don't forget to pay her for a writing job well done.

➤ Has your child read every available book on her favorite topic? If she still wants more, take her to a university library or help her to find more books through the interlibrary loan system at your public library. This is a free service; libraries can usually order any book in print, and the loan period is often longer than two weeks.

➤ Have your child plan a treasure hunt with one clue leading to another and finally to a big surprise. Clues can be rhymes or riddles if your child is so inclined. Help your first grader think about her audience (who is going on the hunt?) and plan the treat at the end.

If your child is ready to read chapter books, here are a few that you won't want to miss.

CHAPTER BOOKS

Amber Brown Is Not a Crayon, You Can't Eat Your Chicken Pox, Amber Brown, and more, by Paula Danzinger (Scholastic)

Catwings and *Catwings Return,* by Ursula K. LeGuin (Scholastic)

Go Fish, by Mary Stoltz (HarperCollins)

Junie B. Jones and the Stupid Smelly Bus, Junie B. Jones and the Yucky Blucky Fruitcake, and more by Barbara Park (Random House). Junie, a five-year-old, uses younger speech patterns such as "bestest" and "hidded," but she and the stories are hysterical, and first graders love looking back on who they used to be.

Marvin Redpost: Kidnapped at Birth? Marvin Redpost: Is He a Girl? and more, by Louis Sachar (Random House)

The Missing Fossil Mystery, by Emily Herman (Hyperion)

Pirate's Promise, Shoeshine Girl, The Chalk Box Kid, White Bird, and more, by Clyde Robert Bulla (Random House)

Sarah Plain, and Tall; and *Skylark,* by Patricia MacLachlan (HarperCollins)

The Stories Julian Tells and *More Stories Julian Tells,* by Ann Cameron (Farrar Straus & Giroux)

Just So Stories, by Rudyard Kipling (Morrow)

Math Exercises

Geometry

The ability to recognize geometrical shapes is measured by question 1 of the Math Assessment.

Knowing the colors and the basic geometrical shapes has long been regarded as a prerequisite for school. Why basic shapes? Because the ability to identify basic shapes signals a readiness for other skills. In order to name the shapes, a child must differentiate between a shape with three corners and three sides and another shape that has four corners and four sides. This kind of visual discrimination also allows your child to recognize and name other symbols, specifically letters and numbers.

But there are other reasons for learning about basic shapes. Working with shapes gives children practice in categorizing and sorting—a skill that is necessary to all mathematical learning. And basic shapes are a foundation of geometry, which is the measurement and relationship of forms in our physical world. If your child has plenty of practice with forms and spatial awareness now, she will be able to build upon this knowledge and apply it for years to come.

If your child is unable to name the shapes, there are two questions for you to consider: (1) Can my child differentiate between the different forms? and (2) Does my child need more practice in recalling the names of the shapes?

The following activities will help you determine the answers to these questions and assist your child in developing a more thorough understanding of how shapes are identified. Be aware, however, that most five-year-olds cannot draw the slanted line in a triangle; this skill does not usually develop until a child is at least five and a half. If your child cannot draw a triangle, chances are she simply needs more maturation time.

HAVE FIVE MINUTES?

➤ Give your child a pile of toothpicks. Ask, "What closed shapes can you make?" Tell her that if a marble is placed in the center of a closed shape, it will have no way out, whereas an open shape would allow the marble to escape. Allow your child to make any shapes she can come up with. Then ask her to tell you how many corners and how many sides each shape has.

Next, have her show you a square. If she needs help, tell her that a square has four corners and four sides. Let her experiment until she comes up with a form that fits this description. If she makes a rectangle, explain that a square is a special kind of rectangle with all sides the same length.

Remove some of the toothpicks to show your first grader a square.

Repeat this activity, inviting your child to make triangles. Show her that triangles can look different from each other as long as they have three corners and three sides. Then ask your child to make a circle (no corners, no sides). When she realizes that it is impossible to make a circle from toothpicks, offer her a string.

➤ Search for shapes inside your home. What shape is a window? A drain? A coat hanger? You may want to record the number of shapes you find. After searching for shapes in one room, ask, "Which shape do you think we'll find most often in the kitchen? The living room? Upstairs?"

➤ Cut assorted shapes of different sizes from construction paper. Have your child create a picture by gluing the shapes onto a sheet of paper. Encourage her to tell you about her picture and the shapes she used.

➤ Show your child an assortment of three-dimensional shapes such as an orange, a block, a paper towel tube, a rectangular box. Invite her to categorize the objects according to those that can roll and those that cannot. Then have her categorize the shapes by those that can be stacked up and those that cannot. Point out that a cylinder such as a paper towel tube can roll or be stacked depending on how it is placed.

➤ Give your child a wooden block, a small rectangular box, a plastic cup, and something with a pyramid shape if you have it. Have her trace one surface of each object on a sheet of paper to discover the basic shapes. Then invite her to look at more objects around the room and predict the two-dimensional shape that will appear on the paper when she traces the object. What shapes can she name?

➤ Go to a playground to search for shapes. Reinforce your child's growing knowledge: "You're right. A triangle has three sides and three corners. Can you find another triangle?"

➤ Make a shape path. Using chalk on your driveway or sidewalk, or drawing on a strip of butcher paper, make a path with circles, triangles, and squares drawn fairly close together. Challenge your first grader: "Can you walk this path by stepping on circles only? Squares only? Triangles only?"

➤ Help your child make a shape mobile. Cut out shapes from tagboard. Using glue, glitter, ribbon, markers, buttons, and anything else you can think of, decorate the shapes together. Then, using string, hang the shapes from a coat hanger, a tree branch, or a paper plate.

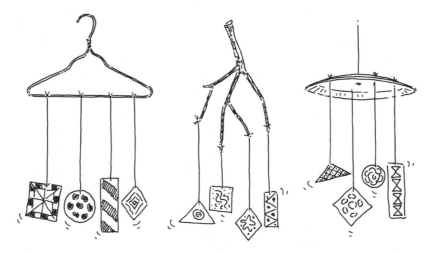

➤ Give your child a paper plate and some magazines that contain pictures of food. Encourage her to cut out foods that are in the shape of a circle, a square, a rectangle, and a triangle and glue them to the paper plate. If he can't find a shape, suggest he cut a food portion out in the needed shape—a triangle of mashed potatoes, perhaps.

Sorting and Classifying

The ability to sort and classify is measured by question 2 on the Math Assessment.

Mathematics and logical thinking are both built upon the understanding that objects have attributes and can be sorted, counted, and classified according to these attributes. While learning to sort and classify, your child will be developing his reasoning skills—skills that will serve him well in algebra, geometry, calculus, and statistics as well as in *all* other school subjects.

HAVE FIVE MINUTES?

➤ Suggest that your child sort the unmatched socks, put the clean silverware away, or separate the pens that work from those that do not work.

➤ Ask your child to help you put away the groceries. Ask which food items go in this cupboard? Which foods go in the refrigerator? The freezer? Then ask, "Why are some foods stored in the refrigerator and some foods stored outside the refrigerator?" Help your child realize that the foods are sorted according to temperature.

➤ Play pairs. On a table or a rug, randomly place a group of objects that can be sorted in pairs. For instance, you might use a hat and a mitten, a nail and a screw, a needle and thread, and a key and a key ring. Invite your child to match the objects. He may find the pairs you were thinking of, or he may match the objects differently. If he does, ask him to tell you his rules for sorting. He may have very reasonable matches. For instance, he may match the key ring and the nail because you hang your keys on a nail. The key and screw might go together because "both turn." Praise him for his creative thinking. There are no right and wrong answers in this game.

➤ Give your child a pile of objects such as keys, buttons, toy cars, or jewelry. Ask him to sort the objects into groups. When he is finished, ask him to tell you the rule he used for sorting. Praise this rule, and then ask if he can sort them by a new rule. For instance, buttons could be sorted by color, shape, material, size, or the number of holes.

➤ Have your child cut pictures from magazines and sort them into groups. Guess the rule your child used for sorting. If you have time, have her glue the pictures onto different sheets of paper.

➤ Many first graders have collections. Perhaps your child has begun collecting action figures, bean bags, key chains, toy cars, baseball cards, or other objects. Suggest that he sort his collection in a number of ways and record these classifications in his own book. Your child could write headings and list or draw pictures below each heading.

➤ Here's your chance! Have your child sort messy cupboards, shelves, closets (remember all those shoes?), or drawers. Allow your child to determine how the objects will be grouped. You may be pleasantly surprised by the results! Remember, however, that your child will have far more motivation if the mess he's sorting is not in his own room.

➤ Place a Hula Hoop on the floor (Later, when your child is using Venn diagrams, circular diagrams used for sorting, he will remember the Hula Hoop.) Place one group of objects inside the hoop, another group outside. For instance, you might place children's books inside the hoop and grown-up books outside the hoop. Have your child guess your rule for sorting. Then trade roles.

Patterns

The ability to recognize, extend, and create patterns is measured by questions 3, 4, and 5 on the Math Assessment.

What do patterns have to do with math? Everything! Too often, math is thought of as computation, or as a process of memorizing math facts and operations. But math is so much more. Mathematics is a number system of fascinating patterns and relationships. Quite often the search for the answer to a mathematical problem is the search for a pattern. Good teachers recognize this. In addition to teaching children arithmetic, they aspire to give children a thorough understanding of and appreciation for the beauty and magic of numbers and an awareness of mathematics in the world around them.

Here is an assortment of activities to help your child explore and gain a greater understanding of pattern. They progress from simple patterns to more complex patterns involving symbols.

One note: If you had difficulty with math when you were in school, try not to communicate this to your child. Instead, participate in some of these activities and discover the fun of math.

HAVE FIVE MINUTES?

➤ Clap your hands and stamp your feet to a simple pattern. Have your child repeat the pattern. Begin with an AB pattern such as: clap, stamp, clap, stamp. Then move to an ABB pattern: clap, stamp, stamp, clap, stamp, stamp; or an AABB pattern: clap, clap, stamp, stamp. Invite your child to make up a pattern for you to follow.

➤ Empty your junk drawer and take turns making simple patterns from what's available. When you've played this game several times, vary it by making an error when it's your turn. Challenge your child to catch your mistake.

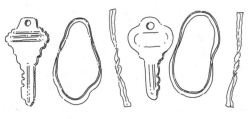

➤ Do you have a set of colored wooden beads and a string? Have your child string a patterned necklace.

➤ Hunt for patterns in your home—in fabrics, floors, wall coverings, ornate boxes, and jewelry. You'll be amazed at how many different patterns you find. Suggest that your child draw one of the patterns on paper.

➤ Write a list of sequential numbers in the twenties, thirties, or forties. Have your child look for a pattern. She will probably notice that all of the numbers in the left-hand column are the same and that the numbers in the right-hand column increase by one. This activity may seem too simple for a child who can probably count to 100. But being able to count the numbers and actually visualizing them (or having any real understanding of their quantity) are two separate things. Activities such as this will give her more hooks for learning.

HAVE MORE TIME?

➤ Buy colored modeling clay. Have your child make clay beads of different shapes and colors and string them. Perhaps your child's necklace will focus on only one attribute—shape—as in square, circle, square, circle. Or on two attributes: red square, blue square, yellow circle, blue circle, red square. If you don't have access to clay, your child can string pasta of different shapes and colors.

➤Using objects such as toothpicks, paper clips, raisins, beans, noodles, or coins, make round designs. You may want to call them flowers or snowflakes to help your child get started. Give your child plenty of practice in making these patterns and watch how elaborate and beautiful they get!

➤Provide your child with fabric markers and a T-shirt, socks or a cloth napkin. Suggest he make a pattern around the edges or, if he's ambitious, over the entire cloth.

➤Make pattern grids. Begin with a small grid, perhaps six boxes wide and six boxes tall. Have your child write his name over and over, from left to right, inside the grid. Then have him search for patterns. In this grid there are some obvious vertical patterns. But in other grids, you might notice a diagonal of all the same letters. Or three letters that are repeated throughout, like the KER in this grid. You can make grids with letters, numbers, or shapes. Have your child assign a color to each symbol and then color the grid. This will make the patterns more apparent.

E	r	i	K	E	r
i	K	E	r	i	k
E	r	i	K	E	r
i	K	E	r	i	K
E	r	i	K	E	r
i	K	E	r	i	K

➤Search for these books that help teach children about patterning: *The Goat in the Rug*, by Charles L. Blood and Martin A. Link (Simon & Schuster) and *A Cloak for the Dreamer*, by Aileen Friedman (Scholastic).

Number

The ability to understand number is measured by questions 6, 7, 8, 9, 10, 11, 12, 13, 24, and 26 on the assessment.

When working with numbers, first graders often appear more precocious than they are. Many can count to 40, 50, and beyond. But ask them to count the number of objects on the table and they miss one object altogether and count two others twice. If you show them a pile of six objects and ask how many they see, they may count and give you a correct answer. But if you rearrange the same six objects and repeat the question, the first grader may count the objects all over again. He does not recognize the constancy of numbers. Or you may ask a first grader to estimate the number of beans in a pile on the table, and he may guess 9, 20, or 58. Numbers are all the same to him.

In other words, first graders often count by rote without truly understanding the nature or quantity of numbers. This is one reason why children need to spend a great deal of time working with real objects, or math manipulatives, as they are called in some classrooms. First graders who do not spend time working with concrete materials and focus instead on paper-and-pencil arithmetic are likely to memorize rules and procedures without gaining a genuine understanding of mathematics. Children who are shortchanged in this way will certainly be the ones saying "I don't get it" later on.

HAVE FIVE MINUTES?

➤Engage your child in real counting experiences every day. *How many spoons do we need at the table? How many eggs are left in the carton? How many of these shirts still fit you? How many stuffed animals are on your bed now?* Occasionally ask a question in which the answer is zero to help your child develop the concept of this number. Say, for example, "How many glasses are on the table?" When he says, "None," you can reply, "Oh. There are zero glasses on the table."

➤Ask, "How many times can you jump?" Count together as your child jumps around the room. This helps reinforce the concept of one-one correspondence (one jump for each number). Vary the game by counting hops, skips, or claps. Or on the quiet side, count how many times he sticks his tongue out, blinks, or does a toothbrush stroke.

➤ Photocopy the Number Race page at the back of this book (page 190). Your child rolls a number cube or die and colors in a box for the number rolled. Have her keep rolling. Which number will win the race by having all of its boxes colored in first?

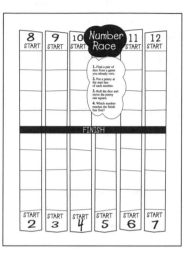

➤ Cut off two cups from one end of an empty egg carton. Now you have a ten-frame. Using marbles, toy cars, or pennies, have your child show you a number from one to ten by placing one object inside the egg carton. Have him fill up one row before placing objects in the next. Seeing objects arranged in this way will help reinforce one-one correspondence and will help your child as he uses addition strategies and place value. When your child becomes more familiar with counting, ask him to show you numbers in the teens. Have him fill up the ten-frame and place the extras outside.

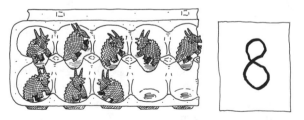

➤ Familiarize your child with the meaning of the words *more, fewer, less*. Ask, "How many steps does it take you to get upstairs?" Then say, "Can you get up stairs using fewer steps?" And when your child gives you a new total, ask, "How many fewer steps is that?" Repeat the activity having your child make the climb with more steps.

➤ Give your child a pile of small objects. Say, "Show me two more than five. Show me one more than eight."

➤ Teach your child the language of ordinal numbers. Line up a group of objects such as toy animals. Say, rabbit is first, horse is second. Then ask your child questions such as *"Which one is third in line? Can you place bear fifth in line?"* When your child is planning an activity, ask: *"What will you do first? What will you do second?"* Or after reading a story: *"What did the monkey do first?"*

➤ Use a calculator to play What's One More? Show your child how to add one on the calculator. Begin with the number 1. Ask, *"What's one more?"* If she can, have her predict what the number will be before she pushes the buttons. Continue the game for as long as your child is able and willing.

➤ Talk about numbers. At the dinner table, ask everyone to tell you about the number six:
"I'm six," your first grader shouts.
"There were six candles on your cake."
"My birthday is in the sixth month,"
"There are six cans in a six-pack of soda."
"Look, I have six features on my face." Child points to two eyes, one nose, one mouth, and two ears.
"Half of six is three."
Take turns choosing numbers to discuss, but don't forget zero. You'll find that it's a favorite to think about.

➤ Give your child ten pennies. Have her shake them up in her hands and drop them on the floor. Are there more heads, more tails, or an equal number of heads and tails?

➤ Hang a calendar over your child's bed. You'll be surprised at how often he studies the pages. Before long, he will have counted the numbers in sequence. He'll have recognized patterns in the teens and twenties. He may even begin to construct problems for himself: How many days until the weekend? How many days until the month is over? How many days until my birthday? Little, Brown sells a reasonably priced "Make Your Own Calendar" for children. Children color their own pictures for each month and are provided with stickers to mark important dates. These calendars can become keepsakes of your child's art each year.

➤ For one whole day record together all of the ways in which numbers are used. Your list might include looking at the clock while getting ready for school, counting the appropriate number of snacks to place in the back-pack, waiting for bus number 22, the number of seconds it takes (counting 1-Mississippi, 2-Mississippi) for the bus to appear—you get the idea. How many ways did you come up with?

➤ Make a chart with the numbers 1 to 5 across the top. Then have your child search for things around the house that equal each number. Do you have four dining room chairs? Write or draw a picture under four. One broom? Record it under one. If this is too simple for your child, write the numbers 6 to 10 or on the chart, challenge her with numbers in the teens! This may take extra time hunting as well as counting.

➤ Give your child handfuls of small objects: dried beans, noodles, paper clips, toothpicks, nuts and bolts. Have him show you the number 6 by arranging the objects in as many ways as he can. Continue this activity at this sitting or at a later time with the numbers 6 to 12.

You might want to glue these arrangements onto separate sheets of paper. Then fasten the sheets together to make number books. Show your child how to write the number he's demonstrating on each page. Or make a book with each page devoted to a different number. Show several arrangements of objects on each page.

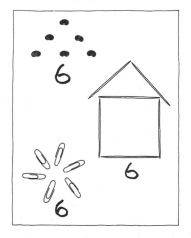

➤ Play a game of dominoes. This gives your child plenty of practice in counting and matching, and it provides your child with a lasting visual image of numbers. Many children, when beginning to calculate simple math problems in their heads, will picture domino or dice patterns in their mind.

➤ Play mancala. There are many versions of this African game on the market, some for under ten dollars. It's well worth the price. Early on, mancala helps reinforce counting and one-one correspondence. As children become more familiar with the game, it sharpens their addition skills and develops their strategic thinking. If you're familiar with mancala, you can make your own game by using the bottom half of an empty egg carton, two extra cups or bowls, and 36 dried beans or pebbles. Place the egg carton horizontally between you and your child. Place an empty cup, or mancala, at either end of the carton. The mancala on your right is yours. Here are the rules:

MANCALA

1. Place 3 beans in each cup of the egg carton, leaving the mancalas empty.
2. Players take turns picking up all the beans from a cup on their side of the carton and moving them counterclockwise, placing one in each cup and mancala along their path.
3. If the last bean lands in their own mancala, they take another turn.
4. If the last bean lands in an empty cup on their side, they put the beans from the opposite cup into their own mancala.
5. When one player has no more beans left on his side of the carton, the game ends. The other player puts all the remaining beans into his or her mancala. The player with the most beans wins.

➤ Have your child go on a scavenger hunt. Make a list asking him to find one thing with the number one on it, two magazines, three books that have the word "the" in the title—and keep going up to ten. Or hold the scavenger hunt outside. Your child can search for pinecones, leaves, scraps of litter. If your child needs a simpler list, make one with pictures. Write numbers next to the pictures.

➤ At snack time, bring out a box of Cheerios or make some popcorn. Give your child three minutes to roll a pair of dice and count out the number of snack pieces indicated by the rolls. If your child throws two ones, however, he needs to return all the snacks to the original pile. At the end of three minutes, invite your hungry first grader to count the total number of snack pieces and gobble them up!

Countless books in libraries and bookstores will help children recognize numbers and count. Here are some notable ones:

Anno's Counting Book, by Mitsumasa Anno (HarperCollins)
Each Orange Had 8 Slices: A Counting Book, by Paul Giganti Jr.
(Greenwillow). (This book also presents the concept of multiplication.)
The Flashing Fireflies, by Philemon Sturges (North South Books)
How Many How Many How Many, by Rick Walton (Candlewick)
Miss Spider's Tea Party, by David Kirk (Scholastic)
One White Sail: A Caribbean Counting Book, by S. T. Garne (Simon &
Schuster)
Splash, by Ann Jonas (Morrow)
Ten Little Rabbits, by Virginia Grossman (Chronicle)

Skip-Counting

The ability to skip-count is measured by question 17 on the Math Assessment.

"I can count to 100 in less than a minute," says a first grader with an impish grin. "One, two, skip a few. Ninety-nine, one hundred."

Most first graders love skip-counting. Although counting by twos, fives, and tens won't get them to 100 as fast as the ditty above, they do feel older and more accomplished as they count off larger numbers. The notion that you can start counting at a number other than one is key to the strategy of "counting on" in addition. Patterns made by skip-counting help children develop strategies for problem-solving, understand the concept of even and odd, and, later, comprehend the basis for division. Knowing how to count by tens and hundreds makes sense of our base-ten place-value system. And, looking ahead, if your child knows how to count by twos, threes, fours, fives, and tens, she will already know nearly half her multiplication tables!

Be aware that most children learn to count by tens first and, later, by fives and twos.

HAVE FIVE MINUTES?

➤ Write the numbers 1 to 10 in a vertical column. Next to this list, write the numbers 10, 20, 30, and so on, to 100. Ask, "What pattern do you see?" With your child, count by tens, pointing to the numbers.

➤ Once your child knows how to count by tens, demonstrate how to count by tens beginning with numbers other than 1. For instance: 6, 16, 26, 36, 46 . . . You may want to write numbers down initially to give your child visual clues. Take turns choosing any number to begin with. Some children love to count by 10 beginning with 100 or 800.

➤ When the whole family is present, ask your child to tell you how many fingers there are in the room. Let your child count in whichever manner he chooses. If he counts by ones, show him how to count by fives or tens, and ask him if the results are the same.

➤ Give your child a pile of pennies. Ask him to organize them so you can count them quickly. Ask, "Is there another way you could arrange them? Which way would be the fastest?"

➤ Show your child how to add up his dimes counting by tens. Show him how to count up his nickels counting by fives.

➤ Teach your child the tally system. Choose a pile of things that need to be put away. For every item your child puts away, have her make a tally mark. Show her how to cross the bundles with the fifth mark. After she has cleaned up the pile, give her a nickel for every five tallies. Encourage her to count up her nickels by fives.

➤ Count together. You say the odd numbers and your child says the even. Before long, your child will be able to count by twos without you.

➤ Using a calculator, have your child add 2 to each number on the keyboard. Suggest he predict what the next number will be before he adds.

HAVE MORE TIME?

➤ Photocopy the 0–99 grid at the back of this book (page 191). Then ask your child to color every tenth, fifth, or second square. What patterns does she see? You may even want to have her try all three on the same

0-99 Grid									
0	1	2	3	4	5	6	7	8	9
10	11	12	13	14	15	16	17	18	19
20	21	22	23	24	25	26	27	28	29
30	31	32	33	34	35	36	37	38	39
40	41	42	43	44	45	46	47	48	49
50	51	52	53	54	55	56	57	58	59
60	61	62	63	64	65	66	67	68	69
70	71	72	73	74	75	76	77	78	79
80	81	82	83	84	85	86	87	88	89
90	91	92	93	94	95	96	97	98	99

grid by coloring every tenth square, circling every fifth square, and putting an x in every second square.

➤ Check out this book from your library: *Arctic Fives Arrive* by Elinor Pinczes (Houghton Mifflin). Have your first grader try counting backwards from fives as the author demonstrates in this story.

Estimating

The ability to estimate is measured by questions 24, 25, and 26 on the Math Assessment.

What is estimation? It is the ability to take the information available to you and think about a reasonable answer. The ability to estimate is a useful math tool. When shopping, we estimate the total price of our purchases. When building, we estimate the amount of each material we need or the time it will take us. When cooking, we estimate how much spaghetti to throw in the pot. Recent research has shown that adults use estimation for more than half of their daily arithmetic needs.

Learning to estimate not only helps children make good decisions but also gives them a genuine understanding of number. Initially, when asked how many beans are in a cup, the first grader may say ten or she may say ten thousand. Only with repeated practice in estimating and counting will she begin to understand what a reasonable answer is. Help your child to see that thinking makes estimating different from guessing.

Later, when your child is doing computations and word problems, she will be able to estimate the answer ahead of time. Knowing whether a final answer is in the ballpark or not is a terrific way to self-correct.

Many first graders want to be "right" or want to "win" when estimating. Show your child that estimations are not exact by estimating yourself and then checking your answer together. For instance, you might say, "I bet I have about thirty-five pages left in this book." (Make sure your estimate is off a bit.) Tell your child how you reasoned out the answer. "Each chapter is about ten pages long, and I have a little over three chapters left." When you determine the exact number, praise yourself for estimating so well. Children who feel free to make rational guesses and be wrong now and then will eventually become better problem-solvers.

In today's world, we rely more and more on statistics. Everything from marketing decisions to policy making is determined by collecting them. Teach your child that numbers, even when they are estimates, can have tremendous influence on how we do things.

HAVE FIVE MINUTES?

➤ First graders love scales. At the grocery store, estimate how many more avocados or mushrooms would make a pound.

➤ While waiting at the doctor's office, estimate the number of minutes you think you will need to wait for your turn.

➤ At the table, have your child estimate how many bites it will take to finish his vegetables, how many sips of milk are in a glass, or how many times the phone will ring during dinner. How close are his estimates?

➤ Your house is full of things to estimate and count. Estimate the number of windows, rugs, or books. How many straws are in the box? How many cans are in the cupboard?

➤ Estimate the number of times your family does something. How many times a day does each family member go up and down the stairs? Open the front door? The refrigerator door? Keep a tally sheet close by to check your estimates.

➤ Ask your child to estimate the number of minutes it takes him to get dressed, put his shoes on, tidy his room. Estimating time is a great way to deal with the dawdling of six-year-olds!

HAVE MORE TIME?

➤ Estimate numbers in the hundreds such as the number of pennies in a jar, or the number of peanuts in a bag. Have your child count them by arranging them in groups of ten. Provide paper cups or small containers to hold the groups.

➤ Read the book *Is a Blue Whale the Biggest Thing There Is?* by Robert E. Wells (Albert Whitman). In addition to learning about number and comparing sizes, you can discuss whether the numbers mentioned in the book are estimated or exact. When is it okay to estimate?

Measurement

The ability to measure objects using nonstandard units and standard units of measurement is determined by questions 22 and 23 on the Math Assessment.

In the ideal first grade classroom, children get lots of practice in measuring in nonstandard units (shoes, beans, hand lengths) and standard units of measurement (rulers, yardsticks, scales).

Why take the time to teach children to measure in nonstandard units? Measuring in nonstandard units teaches children that we can use an infinite number of objects for measuring and comparison. It helps children realize that a ruler is made up of smaller increments lined up in a particular way. Measuring with nonstandard units also shows children how some units are better suited for measuring than others. Would you rather measure an elephant by bean lengths or body lengths? And answers may be different if each child uses his own foot length. Eventually children come to understand the need for standardized units, both metric and nonmetric, and that rulers, yardsticks, and measuring tapes have slightly different uses.

Children in first grade also measure weight and volume by making comparisons. Which weighs more, the stapler or the book? Which holds more, the jar or the box? Since opportunities for this kind of activity are not always available in the school setting, you'll want to provide plenty at home.

HAVE FIVE MINUTES?

> ➤ Have your child compare furniture widths, rug lengths, or room sizes in foot lengths. Show her how to walk, placing one foot carefully in front of the other.

> ➤ Choose a nonstandard but fairly uniform unit such as toothpicks, paper clips, or macaroni. Have your child use this unit to measure different objects. Make sure you show her how to line the units up starting from the base, and having each unit touch. Ask her if she can find something shorter than the object measured. Something longer. Something taller.

> ➤ Ask which is longer, the table or the counter? How can we find out?

> ➤ Have your child choose one object such as a shoe. Have her measure it using a number of different units. Suggest she record and compare her answers. Which unit was the easiest to measure with? Which was the hardest? Why?

> ➤ Give your child something spherical, like a ball. Ask, "How can we measure this?" Let your first grader brainstorm. Guide him to understand that you could measure the object with a string.

> ➤ Give your child a piece of string. Ask him to estimate which objects in the room are longer than the string. Which objects are shorter? Have him measure to check his estimates.

➤ Show your child how to use and read a ruler. Ask her to find something that is 3 inches long, seven inches long, a foot long. Do the same with a metric ruler if you have one.

➤ Ask, "Why do you think rulers have twelve inches and yardsticks have thirty-six inches?"

HAVE MORE TIME?

➤ Help your child measure her different body parts with yarn. Cut off lengths that equal her arm, leg, waist, foot, nose, and finger. Attach a piece of masking tape with the name of the part to each strand. Then have her line the pieces of yarn up, using a baseline, to compare lengths. You've made a graph! Which body part is longest? Which is shortest?

➤ Give your child a real-life reason to measure. Plan a sewing, weaving or building project. Together, estimate and measure the materials you'll need.

Money

The ability to identify the name and value of coins is measured by questions 18, 19, and 20 on the Math Assessment.

There are many concepts to learn about money. Your child's teacher hopes to impart the knowledge that money is an exchange system, that the system comprises coins and paper bills, and that each of these monetary items carries a different value. She will demonstrate that money can be added and subtracted.

You, as a parent, are likely to have your own lessons about money that you wish to teach. Perhaps you want to teach your child how to save money or how to spend money wisely. Both are important, say the experts. We do not develop a healthy balance between spending and saving unless we are given practice in both. You may also want your child to learn more about the relationship between work and money, and you might wish to introduce beginning concepts of banking and interest.

Fortunately, by first grade most children understand the incredible power of money and have a desire to learn more. Knowing the names and denominations of coins and learning to add and subtract money will have a direct influence on a child's ability to make purchases. The desire to save money and to purchase certain items will provide many opportunities for understanding the necessity and value of money.

The most effective way that you can teach your child about money is to give him practice in using it. If you are not giving your child a weekly allowance, you may want to consider doing so now. Or you may want to establish a list of chores your child can do to earn money. Either of these approaches, or a combination of the two, will give your child practice in estimation, place value, computation, and problem-solving skills. Once you have your program under way, try some of the following activities:

HAVE FIVE MINUTES?

➤ Pay your child in different combinations of coins. For instance, if your child receives a dollar each week, give him four quarters one week, ten dimes another. (Eventually you can mix the kinds of coins.) Have him tell you the names of the coins as you count them out. If he can count by tens or fives, have him do so when you present him with his allowance.

➤ Make sure your child has a safe place to keep his money. Suggest from time to time that he take the money out and sort it by coins. Have him tell you the names of the coins and what they're worth.

➤ Suggest that your child save for something special—and reasonable. Initially, he'll have much more success saving for a five-dollar toy than a forty-dollar one. Help him to count his money periodically to see if he has enough. He may not be able to add the larger amounts, but he will learn more about money each time he watches you.

➤ When your child is adding up his money, show him how to add larger values (quarters) first and smaller values (pennies) last.

➤ Give your child money riddles: I have two coins worth 15¢, what are they? I have three coins worth 11¢, what are they? I have four coins worth 28¢, what are they?

➤ Suggest your child trade his money up for larger coins. For instance, he could give you two dimes and a nickel for a quarter.

➤ How many ways can you make twenty-five cents? Help your first grader find the solution to this problem.

HAVE MORE TIME?

➤ Kids love to play store, restaurant, movies, and other fantasy games that involve commerce. You can encourage this kind of play by providing props such as a toy cash register, play money, price labels, take-out menus, or tickets, and you can be a good and steady customer. Writing prices, accepting money, and making change are all excellent ways to build money sense.

➤ Play Monopoly Junior by Parker Brothers. This version of the traditional game is designed specially for children ages five to eight. Although it won't help reinforce coin values, it will give your child practice with, and a better understanding of, the exchange system. Some first graders, however, have been known to insist upon dusting off the family's original Monopoly game and going for Boardwalk!

Time

The ability to tell time to the hour and the half hour is measured by question 21 on the Math Assessment.

Time is a difficult concept for first graders. A true understanding of linear time does not occur until a child's seventh or eighth year. The idea of elapsed time—that is, how long something takes—is usually not well developed until a child's ninth or tenth year. This is perhaps why your first grader displays little understanding of "twenty minutes" and why she is frustrated when you expect her to have certain things done by a certain time. Many six-year-olds seem very sophisticated when they look at a digital clock and tell time. Most really don't have a clue to what those numbers mean.

Time, then, is limited in the first grade to recognizing the hour and the half hour. Occasionally a first grader will show an understanding of minutes, but be cautioned: she may be able to give a correct answer and still not understand that a minute is sixty seconds, an hour is sixty minutes, and so on.

Nevertheless, this is a good time to give your child an analog (not digital) watch. Your first grader will spend a good deal of time studying its face, watching the hands go around, and learning about the patterns of time. Eventually the experience of watching the clock and a more rooted, intuitive understanding of time will come together.

HAVE 300 SECONDS?

➤ Have your child pretend to be a clock. Ask him to stick his tongue, the hour hand, out. Now have him move his tongue around his lips, as you point to a clock and tell the hours. This sounds goofy, but many children assimilate learning if they combine it with body movement.

➤ Have your child use his arms to represent the hour and minute hands. When your child reaches the number 6 with one arm, have him switch arms. Teach him the placement of the hands for each hour. When you are certain that he has mastered this concept, introduce half hours. Have him move his minute arm from the twelve to the six, demonstrating how thirty minutes has passed.

➤ When your child requests something and you can't do it immediately, respond with the hour or half hour in which you can do it: "I can listen to you read at four o'clock," or "We can walk to the store at six-thirty." Have her tell you when it's time.

HAVE MORE TIME?

➤ Make sure your child has a watch or a clock that is not digital. Point out the hour hand and the minute hand. Have her look at the clock repeatedly throughout an hour. What can she tell you about the hands? If you have enough time, have your child draw what she sees each time she looks at the clock.

➤ Make a chart for your child, demonstrating the time that she wakes up, eats breakfast, goes to school, eats dinner, and goes to bed. Show the time on an analog clock and a digital clock.

➤ Make a clock using a paper plate, paper arms, and a brad fastener. Give your child clock problems to solve: What time will it be one hour from now? What time was it two hours ago? What time will it be in a half hour?

➤ Read *My First Book of Time,* by Claire Llewellyn (Dorling Kindersley). This book with photos and a foldout clock is highly recommended. It will introduce your child to the calendar, seasons, and other ways of recording time in addition to teaching her about the analog clock.

Addition and Subtraction

The ability to add and subtract is measured by questions 8, 27, 28, 31, 32, 33, and 34 on the assessment.

When we think of addition and subtraction, we think of endless numbers written vertically or horizontally, with addition signs, minus signs, and equal signs. We may even think of red pen marks circling incorrect answers. We sometimes forget that these papers covered with numbers and signs are not addition and subtraction. They are symbols representing the processes.

You will be giving your child a leg up in mathematics if you take the time to work with concrete materials in real-life situations before turning your attention to math facts on paper or flash cards. Two important concepts are gained while working with real objects:

1. The realization that a number such as 6 is not just a mark that comes after five and before seven, but a group that can be subdivided into parts: $3 + 3, 2 + 4, 1 + 5, 2 + 2 + 2$.

2. An understanding of the relationship between addition (part + part = whole) and subtraction (whole – part = part) and that if you know one addition fact such as $3 + 4 = 7$, then you know another ($4 + 3 = 7$), and you also know two subtraction facts ($7 – 4 = 3$ and $7 – 3 = 4$).

Sometimes teachers and parents try to teach these concepts as tricks. But without real concrete experiences, children cannot hold on to or build upon the knowledge. Eventually there are just too many tricks to remember.

Your first grader will probably spend a good deal of math time this year learning how to add and subtract—first the numbers from 1 to 10, and later the numbers from 10 to 18. Here are some activities to help your child develop an understanding of addition and subtraction. When you've spent a good deal of time doing these activities, and you are convinced that your child is confident in her understanding, go on to Addition Strategies and Subtraction Strategies, which appear later in this chapter.

HAVE FIVE MINUTES?

➤ Using toy animals, toy people or objects as props, take turns telling math stories. For instance you might say, "On the savanna, there were four lions and three zebras. How many animals is that? Well, one evening, just as the sun was setting, there was a thunderous sound. Five of these animals ran for cover. How many animals were left?"

➤ Show your first grader five beans. Ask him to guess how many beans are in your left fist by looking at the remaining beans in your open right hand. Play several times, using different groups. When your child is quick at guessing combinations of five, add one bean at a time until your child can play up to combinations of 10.

➤ Give your child a pile of small blocks. Ask him to show you one more than seven, two fewer than eleven, four more than three. "Show me double the amount of these blocks. Show me the number nine. How many did you add?"

➤ Next time you're on a long car trip, have your child play the animal game. Encourage her to watch for animals out the window. Tell her that she receives one point for every dog, cat, or bird she sees and five points for every cow and horse. All other animals are worth ten points. Have her add the points as you drive along. Only watch out! If you pass a cemetery all animal points are wiped out. If you have two children, they can play this game competitively.

HAVE MORE TIME?

➤ Give your child ten pennies. Say, "Making two groups, how many ways can you show ten?" You might want to give your child some examples. Show her one group of six and one group of four. Then show her one group of three and one group of seven. If your child enjoys this exercise and would like to take it one step further, suggest she write a number sentence such as $4 + 6 = 10$ or $3 + 7 = 10$ for each combination.

➤ Photocopy the Number Train on page 192 in the back of this book. Have your child roll two number cubes or dice and add the numbers together. Then have him color the car that equals the total. How fast can he color the train? (He needs to roll again if the total has already been colored.) When your child has played this game once or twice, suggest that he can add or *subtract* the numbers on the dice. Now how fast can he color the train? For a variation, make a grid 6 boxes wide and 6 boxes high. Write the numbers 1 to 6 at the bottom. Have your child roll a die. If he rolls a 4, he may color in a box above the 4, 2 boxes above the 2, or 1 box above the 1 and 1 box above the three. How fast can he color the entire grid?

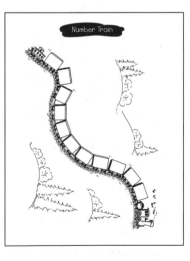

Number Train

➤ Place ten straws or other objects in a pile. Alternate picking up one or two straws on a turn. The person who picks up the last straw wins. Repeat this activity often to help your child develop her logical thinking and a true understanding of subtraction. For a variation, change the number of straws or change the rules so that the person who picks up the last straw loses.

➤ Play a game of dominoes. But before you may add a piece, you must add the sum of the two boxes touching. The next time you play, make it a subtraction game. Subtract the smaller number from the larger number before adding the piece.

Word Problems

The ability to solve word problems is measured by questions 27, 28, and 29 on the Math Assessment.

Unlike geometry or measurement, word problems are not a separate mathematical strand of learning. Word problems are an essential thread of every strand. In other words, whenever you teach your child about shapes, patterns, time, measurement, addition, or subtraction, you are presenting word problems. Word problems are discussed as a separate category here so that you can teach your first grader problem-solving techniques that will support his learning in all areas of math.

As a parent, you are by far the best teacher of problem-solving, because you need not contrive problems. You and your child are faced with actual math problems in a variety of situations every day. Here are three practical word problems:

1. We have five people for breakfast. There are three spoons in the drawer. How many spoons do we need to get out of the dishwasher?
2. The box is a foot long, and the wrapping paper is 15 inches long. Do we have enough paper to wrap the box?
3. I need 8 bagels. The bagels come in packages of 6. How many packages of bagels do I need to buy?

Real problems provide motivation for children to solve them. More importantly, they show children how we use math every day, in every aspect of our lives. While working with problems, children come to realize just how useful math is.

In helping your child sharpen her problem-solving skills, you want to impart a spirit of exploration. Convey that problems can be solved in many ways, and if one strategy doesn't work, she can try another. Emphasize and reinforce her attempts to solve problems rather than correcting her answers. And let her know that some problems are tough and can't be solved immediately.

It also helps to talk to your child about the way she problem solves. Which strategy did she use? How did she do it? Talk to your child about her reasoning when she gets correct as well as incorrect answers.

When your child is solving a problem, suggest she try one of the following strategies: drawing a picture, using objects, acting it out, or looking for patterns.

HAVE FIVE MINUTES?

➤ You can give your child word problems anywhere at any time of day. One way to present word problems automatically is to ask your first grader questions instead of supplying answers: "You got to choose the book on Monday. Your sister got to choose the book on Tuesday. You got to choose on Wednesday. Who gets to choose the book tonight?"

➤ Instead of seeking correct answers, give a word problem. Ask her what she would do to solve the problem. For example, say, "The game you want to buy costs three dollars. You have one dollar. How can you find out how many more dollars you need?" ("I would subtract," "I would draw a picture," and "I would use my play money to figure it out"—all worthy answers.)

➤ Children need to realize that many problems have more than one answer. Ask your child to come up with multiple solutions to problems such as this one: A muffin costs twenty cents. How many different ways could you pay for it?

➤ Give your child an answer and suggest he come up with the problem. For instance, if you gave him the answer five, he might tell you that there were nine rabbits in a hutch but four got loose.

➤ To vary this activity, give your child an answer and suggest he come up with number sentences to represent the problem. The answer five might elicit these responses: $2 + 3$; $2 + 2 + 1$; $7 - 2$.

➤ Ask your child to predict what the answer might be before he solves a problem. Predicting helps him connect the problem to what he already knows. As he gets better at predicting, he will be able to check his answer by comparing it with his prediction.

➤ Pose word problems as ever-popular riddles: If Sarah is two years younger than Kate, and Kate is the same age as an even number between five and seven, how old is Sarah?

HAVE MORE TIME?

➤ Unlike math textbooks, real life seldom gives us all the information we need to solve a problem right away. Chances are, for instance, your child would not know that he had 15 feet of wrapping paper available. Give your child problems that require him to collect data. Ask, "Do we have enough paper to wrap this present? How can we find out?" Here are two other examples:

1. How many shelves will we need to build to hold all your books? (Data needed: How many books does he have? What size will the shelves be? How many books can each shelf hold?)
2. How many desserts do we need to buy for lunches this week? (How many family members will pack a lunch? Will they take it every day? How many days in all?)

Obviously, your child can't make these decisions without your assistance. But presenting and discussing these kinds of problems with your child will create a strong foundation in mathematical thinking.

Addition Strategies

The ability to use addition strategies is measured by questions 31 and 32 on the Math Assessment.

It may appear that there is only one way to add and one way to subtract. On the contrary, good math students use a variety of strategies to solve math problems. Learning these strategies will help your child perform more quickly and confidently. They will also give him or her a more thorough understanding of numbers.

As mentioned, it is always best to teach math concepts with real materials—adding three pennies to five pennies, for example. However, once your first grader thoroughly understands the concept, he should begin to solve math facts by looking at the numbers, recalling a strategy, and *thinking* the problem through. This is called mental arithmetic.

Strategy #1: Counting On

Young children add 4 + 5 by counting four fingers, counting five fingers, and then starting all over again to count to nine. This process gets mighty complicated, especially in working with numbers greater than 10.

Teach your child to "count on" instead: Say "Here's another way to add 4 +

5. Think of the number 4. Now hold up five fingers to count on five." Like this: "*Five, six, seven, eight, nine. The answer is nine.*"

HAVE FIVE MINUTES?

➤ While driving in the car, suggest that your child count on objects. For instance, say: "I see three palm trees [cows, buses, wild hairy camels]. Now I see five more palm trees. How many palm trees is that?" Remind your child to *think* of the first number and count on the second number. As your child gets familiar with the process, continue adding on numbers.

➤ At the grocery store, have your child count on items you place in the grocery chart: "I had six cans in the cart, here are five more. How many cans do we have now?"

➤ Have your child roll number cubes and add the numbers together by counting on. Using number cubes is helpful because children can remember and visualize the dot patterns.

HAVE MORE TIME?

➤ Using chalk on pavement or masking tape on carpet, make a hopscotch grid with the numbers 1 to 18 in order. Give your child an addition problem such as 6 + 8 = ? Have your child begin on the first number and hop on to the answer.

Strategy #2: Double and Doubles Plus One

For some reason we have less difficulty remembering a double fact such as 3 + 3 = 6, than a fact such as 3 + 4 = 7. So first help your child learn doubles (1 + 1 = 2, 2 + 2 = 4, 3 + 3 = 6 . . .) and then try the doubles-plus-one strategy. Say to your child, "Look at this math example: 3 + 4 = ____. What is the closest double?" Your child will answer that 3 + 3 = 6. Now ask him, "How can knowing that double help you solve 3 + 4?" He'll reply, "I can add one! 3 + 3 = 6, so 3 + 4 = 7." Some kids might say the closest double is 4 + 4 = 8. Then they would subtract one. That strategy works just as well.

HAVE FIVE MINUTES?

➤ While eating dinner tonight, have your child show you doubles with her vegetables—4 peas + 4 peas equals 8 peas

➤ Whenever possible, tell your child to "Double it!" How many books did you pick up? Double it! How many minutes did you brush your teeth? Double it! How many cookies did you eat? Double it!

➤ Encourage your child to do small jobs for pay. Make a price list: wipe off table, 4 cents; sort shoes, 6 cents; empty trash, 9 cents. Then offer to double her earnings if she does all the jobs on the list. Have your child compute the doubled prices.

HAVE MORE TIME?

➤ Make a super-duper fact computer. Here's how:

1. Cut two 5-inch, horizontal slots in a half-gallon milk carton—one at the top and one at the bottom, as shown.

2. Open the top. Glue a strip of oaktag inside the carton. Glue the top of the strip directly above the top slot. Glue the bottom of the strip directly below the bottom slot. Have your child decorate the computer if he wishes.

3. Using index cards, make a set of doubles or doubles-plus-one flash cards. Write the problem on one side, the solution on the other.

4. Now have your child choose a card and find the sum. She can check her answer by putting the card into the computer problem side up. The answer will be shown as the card automatically comes out the bottom slot!

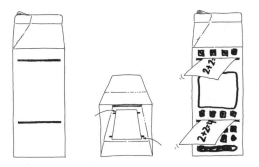

Strategy #3: Make a Ten

This strategy should be introduced when your child can add to 10 fairly quickly and is ready to add numbers to 18.

It will take your first grader no time at all to realize that adding numbers to 10 (10 + 2, 10 + 4) is "way easy." Strategy number 3 is this: whenever you add nine, make a ten.

"Look at this addition sentence: 9 + 5 = ___. What does the nine need to make a ten?"

"One."

"If you take one from five what does that leave you?

"Four."

"What is 10 + 4?"

"Fourteen! Way easy!

As your child becomes more proficient, making a ten when adding numbers other than nine will become way easy, too.

HAVE FIVE MINUTES?

➤ Help your child visualize this strategy: Make a ten-frame with five boxes on top and five on the bottom. Give your child 20 pennies and addition examples that include facts with the number nine. Suggest that your child place nine pennies in the grid, then add the second number by placing one more in the grid and counting the remaining pennies.

$$9+5=14$$

➤ Challenge your child to write all of the nine addition facts from 0 + 9 to 9 + 9. Ask, "Do you see any patterns?" (The ones place in the answer is always one less than the number added to nine.)

➤ While waiting at the dentist's or doctor's office or any other place where there are gossip magazines but your child won't let you read them, call out nines facts to be solved mentally.

HAVE MORE TIME?

➤ Teach this game to two children.

1. Deal an entire deck of cards and have the children place their cards in a pile face down.

2. Children simultaneously turn one card over and find the sum. For instance, if one child turned a four and the other child turned a seven, the sum of the two cards would be 11. The first child to say the sum gets to keep the pair.

3. Aces count as one. Jacks, queens, and kings count as ten. After all the cards have been turned over, the child with the most pairs wins.

VARIATIONS:
- If you don't have two children, have your child race an egg timer or a stopwatch.
- If you have an older child who is learning multiplication, have one child add while the other multiplies. You may want to watch this game!

Subtraction Strategies

The ability to use subtraction strategies is measured by questions 33 and 34 on the Math Assessment.

As your child becomes familiar with strategies, she is bound to develop some of her own. You will be amazed at the mental gymnastics your child can do to come up with an answer. Some of the addition strategies such as "make a ten" work equally well for subtraction. Here are a couple more subtraction strategies to add to her repertoire:

Strategy #1: Count Backwards

This strategy is similar to the "count on" adding strategy, but this time your child begins with the total and counts back. So to solve the problem 7 − 5 = ___ your first grader should start at seven and count back five numbers. She will end at the difference: two.

Some children will use their fingers when counting backwards. This is fine. Most children will give up this strategy, along with counting on their fingers, when they've begun to memorize math facts. Counting on the fingers should be viewed as a bridge rather than a crutch.

HAVE FIVE MINUTES?

➤ Use chains of paper clips to give your child concrete practice with this strategy. For example, to illustrate the problem 16 − 8, make a chain of 16 paper clips. Have your child count the paper clips. Then as you count backward from 16, have her remove 8 paper clips one at a time and count the number of clips remaining on the chain.

➤ Give your child plenty of practice in counting back: There are twelve cookies in the bag. If we eat six, how many will we have left? There are fifteen bulbs to plant. If we plant eight today, how many will be left to plant tomorrow? You need to be ready for school in eighteen minutes. If you spend five minutes getting dressed, how much time will you have for breakfast?

➤ Teach your child the song "Ten in the Bed." Then begin at different numbers. For example, sing, "There were thirteen in the bed, and the little one said, 'Roll over. Roll over.' So they all rolled over and one fell out. There were twelve in the bed . . ."

HAVE MORE TIME?

➤ Using large butcher paper or masking tape, make a floor number line. Give your child subtraction examples such as 9 − 5 = ___. Have him stand on nine and hop back five numbers. He will be standing on his answer.

Strategy #2: Learning Fact Families

Here is a fact family:

$4 + 5 = 9$
$5 + 4 = 9$
$9 − 5 = 4$
$9 − 4 = 5$

If your child has begun to memorize addition facts, use concrete materials to show her how addition and subtraction are related. Point out that if she knows the whole (9) and one part (5), she can tell the other part (4).

"What is the whole?"
"Nine."
"What is the part?"
"Five."
"What plus five equals nine?"
"Four!"

One note of caution: Your first grader may assume that because 5 + 4 has the same answer as 4 + 5, then 9 − 4 and 9 − 5 must have the same answer, too. If this point is confusing for your child, make sure that she gets a lot of practice with concrete objects, so that the number sense behind fact families will become second nature to her *before* she starts memorizing.

HAVE FIVE MINUTES?

➤ Use two sets of small objects to show your child the relationships between the facts in a fact family. This activity works especially well if the two sets are of a different color or shape. Have your child make two groups of objects, each group containing fewer than nine objects. Have her place one set next to the other, and ask her to tell you the addition fact she just demonstrated. Write the corresponding number sentence on paper. Then have your child take away one of the groups. Again have her give you the demonstrated fact, and again write the sentence down. Continue until your child has demonstrated all four facts in the fact family.

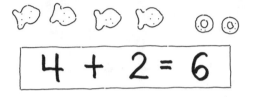

$$4 + 2 = 6$$

> Present a fact family a day. Write three numbers on a card—for instance, 3, 4, and 7. Challenge your child to write four number sentences using the day's numbers (3 + 4 = 7; 4 + 3 = 7; 7 – 4 = 3; 7 – 3 = 4). Eventually, let your child be the one to choose the fact family. Suggest he choose facts that he is having particular difficulty with (often those containing the number 7 or 8).

> Use or make a domino to demonstrate a fact family. Choose a domino such as the 2–3. Place the domino horizontally in front of your child with the 2 to the left, and say, "Two plus three equals what?" Write down the resulting number sentence. Then cover up the two and say, "Five minus two equals what?" Again write down the sentence. Then flip the domino over and repeat the process with 3 + 2 and 5 – 3.

HAVE MORE TIME?

> Give your child a super challenge. Ask, *"How many number sentences with three numbers can you write for the number six, using addition and subtraction?"* If your child enjoys the activity, ask her to predict how many number sentences she can write for larger or smaller numbers.

> Vary this exercise by choosing a number less than six, and inviting your child to use as many numbers in the equation as she wishes. For instance, she could write this sentence for the number six: 2 + 1 + 1 + 2 = 6

> Write the fact families for numbers less than ten. Then give your first grader addition facts such as 3 + 6 = ___. When your child answers the question correctly, reinforce his knowledge by having him cross that sentence, as well as the other three related sentences, off his list of facts to learn.

Place Value
....

The ability to recognize the meaning of tens and ones is measured by questions 14, 15, and 16 on the assessment.

By the *end* of the first grade year your child should begin exploring our ten-based number system. Think about the number 34. It represents 34 individual items. It also represents 3 groups of ten and 4 ones. Eventually children need to learn that the number 3 can mean something altogether different when recorded in different places: 39, 306, 3,303. This is not easy for children to comprehend. In fact many of the problems children have in the upper grades can be traced back to a shaky understanding of place value.

Again, your first grader will require a great deal of experience exploring and practicing place value with the help of concrete materials before she learns the computational tricks of adding or subtracting with regrouping.

In other words, it is perfectly fine to introduce place value by having your child add pennies and dimes in two columns, exchanging pennies for dimes as needed. But it is not advisable to introduce place value by setting up a two-digit addition problem on paper and showing your child how to carry the one. It's not that your child will not succeed in learning this. She will. But you will have taught her a math trick and shortchanged her understanding of how numbers work.

Eventually there are just too many tricks to remember. If your child has been shown how to regroup numbers, ask: "Why did you put a one up here?" If she tells you that she was taught to do it that way, as opposed to telling you that adding the numbers in the ones column makes a new ten, then you know she needs to spend more time working to build a thorough understanding.

For most children, pencil and paper computation that involves regrouping is better left until the second grade. To lay the groundwork try these concrete activities with your first grader:

HAVE FIVE MINUTES?

➤ Provide your child with some paper cups or cupcake papers and a container of small objects such as pennies, macaroni, or paper clips. Have her count the objects by grouping them by tens. Then ask, "How many tens do you have? How many ones? What number does that make?" Write down the number so she can see it on paper.

➤ Choose a date on the calendar your child is looking forward to—a birthday, perhaps, or a holiday or special event—that is at least ten days away. Together, count the number of days until the event. Then, each day between now and that day, place a straw in a small paper bag. When there are ten straws in the bag, have your child bundle them up with a rubber band. Each day, after your child has placed a straw in the bag, have her tell you how many days have gone by. Repeat this activity using events that are at least twenty or thirty days away.

➤ Find a magazine picture that has a multitude of objects: a flock of birds, a pile of blocks, a crowd of people (if you can't find a magazine picture, wrapping paper might do.) Have your child make loops around groups of ten in the picture. How many objects are there in all?

HAVE MORE TIME?

➤ Play One Hundred Beans. For this game you will need a deck of cards with the jacks, queens, and kings removed; ten cupcake papers or small paper cups for each player; and a bag of dried beans. Each player takes a turn choosing a card and placing in front of her the number of beans indicated on the card. If the player can, she makes a group of ten beans in a cup. The remaining beans stay where they are. The first player to reach 100 beans is the winner.

➤ Using your grocery checkout slip, ask your child to compare two different prices with pennies. For instance, tell your child that the lemon you bought cost 49¢. Have her count out pennies (using cupcake papers) to represent this number (4 cups of ten and nine ones). Then have her show you the price of the plum, and ask, "Which cost more? Which number has more tens?"

Math Enrichment

So your child has zoomed through the first grade math curriculum and is ready for more. What now?

Most math teachers agree that unless your child is clearly conceptually gifted, it is better to spend time consolidating and extending this year's learning than to try to teach next year's skills. New concepts such as regrouping (carrying and borrowing) and multiplication can be introduced on the concrete level, using concrete materials, but they should not be introduced on the symbolic level. In this way you will be working with, and not against, your child's cognitive maturation.

Logical thinking, spatial understanding, problem-solving, estimation, probability—all of these can be further developed with the skills your child has mastered. As you and your child explore the problems in this chapter, you'll be helping her to learn, and you'll also be helping her learn how to search for successful solutions.

HAVE FIVE MINUTES?

➤ Look at a magazine advertisement with many objects or people. Ask questions such as how many noses are on this page? How many ears? How many arms and legs? See if your child can find ways to figure out the problem rather than counting objects by ones each time. Your child should begin to develop some multiplication strategies: "There are three people. Each person has two ears. Three groups of two is six."

➤ Search for tessellating patterns. As you may remember, a tessellating pattern is one in which all of the shapes are touching without any white space between them. A checkerboard is a tessellating pattern. Perhaps you can find a tessellating pattern on your bathroom floor, on wallpaper, wrapping paper, or on a walkway.

➤ Challenge your child to make her own balance scale. What materials will she use? How will she make it work? Which objects can she compare with her balance scale?

➤ For a tool in estimating, teach your first grader how to round numbers off to the nearest ten. If the number in the ones place is less than five, you round to the lower ten. If the number in the ones place is five or greater, you round to the higher ten. Then give your child numbers to add mentally after rounding them off. For instance, if this item costs 29¢ and this other item costs 43¢, what do you estimate the total will be? *(After rounding and adding: 70¢.)*

➤ On a sheet of paper, write a list of numbers such as 2, 14, 25, 96, and 1,250. Then ask your first grader some questions: Which number would describe a reasonable number of cookies to eat? Which numbers could be the number of students in a class? Which number would describe the number of beans in a serving? Which number would describe the number of miles to Grammy's house? Which number tells how many hours it would take to get there?

➤ With your child, measure the length of one side of a square or rectangular table. Then ask, "Can you tell me how long the other sides are?" If it's a square, your child should guess the same length. If she doesn't, have her measure. If it's a rectangular table, have her estimate how long the other sides will be. Then check her estimate.

➤ When giving your child math problems to solve, include some that require her to remember the number of days in a week, month, and year and the number of inches in a foot and the number of feet in a yard. For example, ask, *"If there are three weeks until summer vacation, how many days do we need to wait?"*

➤ Give your first grader an imaginary twenty dollars. Have her choose items from a catalog that she could afford to buy with this money. You might want to divide a sheet of paper into two columns labeled tens and ones, and provide your child beans and paper cups to do the addition. Every time she gets ten beans, she places them in a cup and moves them from the ones to the tens column. If this is the case, have her discard the cents and simply add the dollar amounts.

➤ Next time your child is bored, give her a penny to flip. Have her flip it ten times and record how many times it turns up heads and how many times it turns up tails. Ask, *If you do it again, do you think your numbers will be the same?* Have her test her hypothesis. Another time have her flip two pennies at a time.

➤ What is "macaroni" added to "mudpie"? Fourteen! What is "lemonade" added to "chocolate"? Seventeen! Write these words on a slip of paper. Then challenge your first grader to find out how you came up with your answer *(by counting the number of letters in each word and adding them together)*. Once he's figured it out, see if he can find a combination of words whose letters add up to 8, 12, or 24. What's the largest combination he can come up with?

HAVE MORE TIME?

➤ Play these games with your child: Battleship, mancala, checkers, chess, pattern blocks, Chinese checkers, Parcheesi, tangrams, Yahtzee, or Uno.

➤ Photocopy the 0–99 grid at the back of this book (page 191). Then, using pennies, ask her to do the following: put a penny on all the numbers with 2 in them; remove the pennies from the 2's and place them on all the numbers with a 3 in them; all the numbers with a 0 in them; all the numbers with a 5 in the ones place. What patterns does she see? What new rules for marking can your first grader come up with?

0	1	2		4	5	6	7	8	9
10	11	12		14	15	16	17	18	19
20	21	22		24	25	26	27	28	29
40	41	42		44	45	46	47	48	49
50	51	52		54	55	56	57	58	59
60	61	62		64	65	66	67	68	69
70	71	72		74	75	76	77	78	79
80	81	82		84	85	86	87	88	89
90	91	92		94	95	96	97	98	99

➤ Invite your child to make a map of a room in your house. Explain that a map is a bird's-eye view, and that objects such as furniture will appear as one-dimensional shapes such as circles, squares, and rectangles. (Many six-year-olds will still draw maps with drawings that look like the objects, and that's okay. This is one of those concepts that comes with maturation.)

➤ Help your first grader make a calendar page for this month. Then have her make a list of Tuesday dates, Wednesday dates, and Saturday dates. Can she see a pattern?

➤ Play "Nines" on a calculator. Begin with 0. Each player takes turns adding 1 or 2 into the calculator. The first player to reach 9 is the winner. Going over 9 loses. Play this game several times to give your first grader a chance to develop a strategy. Then try reversing the game, beginning at 9 and subtracting 1 or 2 at each turn to see who gets to 0 first.

➤ Have your child roll two number cubes, add the sum and record the total. Ask, "If you keep doing that, which sum will you get most often?" Have her roll the cubes and add for ten minutes to test her estimate. Ask, "Which sum came up most often? Which sum came up least often? Why?" In asking these questions you will help your child explore the concept of probability.

➤ Introduce magic squares to your child. A magic square is a 3x3 grid with numbers in each box. If you add the numbers horizontally, vertically or diagonally, the sums are all the same. Here is an example:

4	9	2
3	5	7
8	1	6

➤ Show your child a magic square with some of the numbers missing. Can she complete the square? Here are some examples:

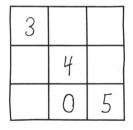
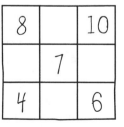

➤ See if your child can make up her own magic square!

Working with Your Child's Teacher

This book and the accompanying assessment can provide you with lots of information about first grade expectations and how your own child is progressing toward meeting those expectations. There is, however, much information about your child's schooling that this book cannot provide.

This book cannot tell you the methods your child's teacher uses to teach first grade skills. Does she teach to the large group, to small groups, or to individuals? Does she encourage children to work together, or does she ask children to work alone? The book also cannot tell you the sequence in which the skills will be taught or integrated into the curriculum. Will measurement be introduced in the beginning of the year or at the end? What math skills will be incorporated into the unit on Japan?

No book can tell you exactly how your child's performance is being measured and recorded this year. Assessment methods vary greatly from school to school and from classroom to classroom. Nor can the book give you a clear picture of how your child interacts in the classroom—you may discover that your child behaves quite differently in a different setting—or how your child is doing socially. Both of these factors greatly affect school success.

To gather the kind of information you need, you must form a strong line of communication between you and your child's teacher. Most schools provide several ways for teachers and parents to share information; however, you may discover that you will glean far more information if you take the lead now and then. Here are some ways that you get a closer look at your child's learning experience.

Open House

Open house, also known as parents' night or back-to-school night, is an evening most schools set aside for teachers to present their goals, methods of instruction, and routines to the children's parents. The purpose of this event, as teachers and administrators are quick to remind parents each year, is not to discuss individual students but to introduce the program and class as a whole.

Open house presentations are as varied as the personalities of teachers who give them. Your child's teacher may present you with a brief written description of his expectations, or he may simply invite you to come into the room and look around. He may have you participate in some of the math and reading activities that the children do, or he may even prepare a video or a slide show to demonstrate a typical day in first grade.

If your child's teacher has not prepared an elaborate or particularly detailed presentation, do remember that not all teachers are extroverts. Many feel far more comfortable in a room with twenty-five rambunctious six-year-olds than in front of a group of adults. If this is the case, posing a few encouraging questions can help the teacher provide you and other appreciative parents more detailed information.

"But," you might say, "what if I am not an extrovert, either? And besides, I don't want the teacher to think I'm an overbearing or uncooperative parent." Indeed, many parents find that they are more anxious on parent's night than the teachers are. A parent's own experiences as a student or lingering fear of authority may cause trepidation. After all, whose heart doesn't beat a little faster at the thought of being sent to the principal's office? Simply meeting the person with whom your child will spend over 180 days this year can be unnerving enough to cause you to sit passively at your child's desk.

Keep in mind that *how* you pose your questions can make a difference. Questions need not be challenges. They can be invitations. "What do land forms have to do with addition and subtraction?" is a challenge. "Your study of land forms sounds fascinating. Can you tell us more about how you will integrate math skills?" on the other hand, is an invitation to discussion. Most teachers are passionate about children and about the subjects they teach. Encourage your child's teacher to expound on what excites him most.

Parent Conferences

There are three kinds of parent-teacher conferences: regularly scheduled conferences, special conferences that you initiate, and special conferences that your teacher initiates. The purpose of each of these conferences is the same: to discuss how your child is doing and how you can support her educationally. Your role in each of these conferences, however, may vary depending upon who initiated the conference.

Regularly Scheduled Conferences

Two scheduled conferences, arranged between you and your child's teacher, usually occur during each school year—one at the beginning of the school year and one later in the year. Before attending the conference, gather some data. Remember, the more information you have going into a conference, the easier the conference will be for everyone. Begin by asking your child for information. Choose a casual time and ask specific questions. A general question like "How's school going?" may not elicit much of a response. Specific questions like the ones below, however, can prompt a response that you will want to follow up on:

- What books are you reading in school?
- Have you had a chance to work on a story lately?
- What do you like best (or least) about math?
- Does your teacher call on you very often?
- What don't you like about school?

Next, think about learning activities you and your child have done together, and any questions the activities have raised. If you have given your child the assessment in this book, you may find that you already have a number of questions. For instance, you may have observed that your child approaches math problems by recalling a procedure: First I do this. Then I do this. Even if the teacher reports that your child is doing well in math, you might want to discuss whether your child is memorizing ways to solve problems or whether he truly understands the way numbers work. Give the teacher some examples of what you have observed at home, and note if your observations match the teacher's.

As you prepare the questions you wish to ask your child's teacher, be aware that the teacher herself is preparing to meet with more than twenty sets of parents. It is likely that she has established a routine such as showing you samples of your child's work or results of formal and informal assessments. She may have one or two issues she wishes to bring to your attention. Due to the uniformity of these conferences, you might find yourself wondering if the teacher truly knows your child. A comment such as "Your son is such a pleasure to have in class" is nice to hear. But it is not nearly as useful—and ultimately as cherished—as "Your son has read all of the beginning mysteries in the classroom and is now gobbling up books about space." To elicit more specific comments about your child, feel free to ask questions about him as an individual. Here are some suggestions:

- In what areas have you seen the most growth and the least improvement?
- How does my child's performance compare to that of other children at this grade level? (Teachers understandably do not wish to compare children and are often reluctant to answer this last question, but it is an important one. Keep in mind that you need to know about your child's progress and performance. The teacher may tell you that your child is growing daily as a reader. However, until you know that that growth is taking place in the lowest reading group, you have only half of the picture.)
- What are my child's work habits like?
- What are my child's interests?
- What motivates my child in school?
- Does my child have special friends?
- How would you describe my child's attention span?
- What can I do at home to support my child's learning?

If during the conference the teacher uses jargon you're not familiar with or if she describes your child in ways that seem vague, ask for clarification. "He's a live wire," for instance, could mean that your child is bright and curious or that he has difficulty sitting still or paying attention. Try not to leave the conference until you are sure you have a clear picture.

Most routine conferences are scheduled in fifteen- to twenty-minute blocks—which is why you want to be on time for yours! If your conference is coming to an end and you have just unearthed an area of concern, ask to schedule another conference. Most teachers will be happy to do so.

You may find that your child is invited or expected to attend your conference with you. This format has both advantages and disadvantages. On the one hand, by attending the conference, your child will be encouraged to take a more active role in his own learning and assessment. On the other hand, you may find that you have questions you would like to discuss with the teacher privately. If your child has been asked to attend and you do not want to discuss all of your concerns in his presence, request a second conference time or indicate that you will be following up with a phone call.

Conferences Initiated by the Parent

Although you may be tempted to gather information from the teacher during a class field trip or when you drop your child off after a dentist appointment, try to refrain from doing so. Impromptu discussions about one child's progress are too much to ask of a teacher who is fully immersed in teaching. Instead, if you have concerns or wish to know more about your child's learning, make an appointment to see the teacher or to speak with her on the telephone.

You may want to schedule a conference or phone call to inform the teacher of any stresses or special circumstances your child is experiencing. Illness, parental separation or divorce, death of a dear one (including a pet), or particular fears can all affect a child's school experience and are well worth sharing with the teacher. It is also appropriate to schedule a conference if you have noticed puzzling changes in your child's behavior. Together, you and the teacher may be able to pull together enough information to make sense of such changes.

Sometimes your concerns will have less to do with your child's individual progress than with the classroom situation as a whole. Perhaps you take issue with a specific method your child's teacher is using, or maybe you would like to see learning addressed in other ways. Parents often hesitate to talk to teachers about these considerations for fear that the teacher will feel attacked and subsequently take the anger out on their child. This common fear is rarely warranted. Teachers know that listening and responding to parents ultimately brings about more support, not less. In most situations a concern, particularly a first-time concern, is taken quite seriously. In schools, as in other institutions, the squeaky wheel does get the grease. Scheduling a conference and voicing your concerns in a genuine spirit of collaboration is appropriate.

If you have a concern about your child and are wondering if you should set up a conference, do so, and do it now. October is not too soon. It is far better to communicate early when both you and your child's teacher can be proactive rather than reactive. Address the problem *before* your child experiences frustration or a sense of failure. Success is the leading motivator in school achievement. Don't let your child lose that feeling of success.

Conferences Initiated by the Teacher

Suppose you come home from work to find a message on your answering machine. Your child's teacher wants to have a conference with you. Like any parent, you assume the worst. First comes the flood of questions for your child: How are things going at school? Any problems? Next comes the steady flow of parent guilt: What have I failed to do?

Don't panic. Call to find out the specific purpose of the meeting. Who knows? Your child's teacher may simply want to talk to you about a volunteer position in the classroom or about your child's special talents. If the teacher seems reluctant to give you details before the meeting, understand that this is to prevent an immediate and full-range discussion at the time of the phone call.

In truth, it is probably more advantageous for everyone involved to wait, process the information, and be prepared at the meeting. To find out the purpose of the meeting, you might say, "I know that we don't have time to discuss the issue now, but could you tell me in a few words what the conference will be about?" Then ask who, other than the teacher, will be attending the conference. Finally, ask, "Is there a helpful way that I can prepare?" This last question will set the right tone, indicating that you are open and eager to work together.

If two parents are involved in your child's education, try to arrange for both of you to attend the conference. This way one parent will not end up trying to communicate information secondhand, and everyone can become involved in a plan of action. Be sure to arrange a means for following up as well. You may want to set up a regular system of communication—sending notes back and forth, for example, or calling every Friday. Some teachers even suggest keeping a dialogue journal in which the parent and teacher exchange progress reports and observations in a notebook that the child carries to and from school.

Whether you or the teacher initiates a conference, remember that the main purpose is to collect and share essential information. More often than not, teachers are relieved when parents bring problems to their attention. You, too, should be glad that a problem has been noticed and addressed. At the very least, by opening a vital line of communication, you and the teacher will clarify important views pertaining to the education of your child.

Student Assessment

When you went to school there were probably only two types of assessments: tests and report cards. The same holds true for many schools today. In some schools, primary students do not take tests, except perhaps a weekly spelling test, but they do get a report card. The report card may have letter grades; it may be a checklist; or it might be an anecdotal report. In still other schools new methods of assessment, called performance-based testing or authentic assessment, use anecdotal records, learning journals, and portfolios as a means of reporting progress. These assessment methods look at learning from one or more angles, and all can be helpful to you and your child if you understand their benefits and limitations.

Report Cards

Report cards are often considered a final evaluation: How well did your child do this quarter? How hard did she try? Many types of report cards, however, raise more questions than they answer. If your child gets letter grades, you may find yourself wondering what a B really means. Is your child performing slightly above average for the whole class? Or is your child performing slightly above average in her math group? Can a child in the lowest math group get a B? If your child doesn't get traditional letter grades, but receives an O for outstanding, S for satisfactory, and an N for needs improvement, you may still be left wondering what constitutes an outstanding grade as opposed to a satisfactory grade.

Some schools are moving toward more informative report cards. These usually include a checklist of skills and learning behaviors and are marked according to how often your child exhibits those behaviors—consistently, most of the time, sometimes, not yet. The checklist may be accompanied by anecdotal records.

Remember, the perfect reporting device for all children has yet to be devised. Report cards are designed for parents, so if the reports in your school do not meet your needs, let the principal know.

No matter what type of report card your child receives, try to use it as a springboard rather than a conclusion. As a springboard, a report card gives you the opportunity to talk with your child. Here are some suggestions:

- First and foremost, praise your child for things done well. In fact, you may want to concentrate only on the positive in your first reaction to a report card.
- Ask your child what she thinks of this progress report. Listen to your child's feelings and guide her in assessing how well she thinks she's doing.
- If you and your child can see an area that needs improvement, talk about *how* your child can go about improving. Telling your child to try harder, or giving her an incentive to do so—say, a dollar for every A—will probably not be helpful. Your child cannot improve without a clear understanding of what is expected of her and how to work on the problem. If you have already pinpointed a need using the assessment in this book, the report card can provide an opportunity to reinforce the good work you have already begun to do together.
- If you and your child have questions about the report card or need further clarification, schedule a conference with your child's teacher.

Above all, keep your discussion with your child as upbeat and positive as possible. Remember, report cards can tear down what your child needs most—confidence. So as your child's main coach, review the report card but don't let it define her. Your child is not an A or a C student. She is what we all are, a continuous learner.

Performance-Based Assessment

In many schools, teachers are pushing for changes in assessment. They realize that learning does not occur only at the end of a unit or the end of a marking period; it is happening all the time. In these schools teachers are keeping records while observing children at work. They talk to children about what they know and how they approach problems. In addition, students and their teachers often collect work that demonstrates learning and keep it in a *portfolio.*

A portfolio is a collection of work. It may contain several writing samples—usually the rough drafts as well as the finished product, to show growth—charts and descriptions that show how a child approached a math or science project, drawings and other artwork, and a report or project done over time. Sometimes the teacher chooses what will go in the portfolio, sometimes the child, and sometimes both. In any case, the student is usually asked to do some self-assessment.

Most parents find portfolios a good source of information about their child's progress and school expectations. They are able to see the quality of their child's thinking, the effort that was applied, and the outcomes. While reviewing a portfolio, parents and teachers can discuss future goals for the child.

If your child's teacher isn't using a portfolio method but sends home completed work regularly, study the work for signs of how she is progressing. Go beyond the teacher's comments at the top of the paper, and look instead for changes you see your child making in her work. Praise her for applying new concepts and showing what she knows. You may even find it useful to keep your own portfolio at home. As you do the exercises in this book, keep work that demonstrates growth. These may come in handy when discussing your child's needs with the teacher.

Standardized Tests

Standardized tests have been administered to children as early as kindergarten. However, many education experts consider the validity of the tests less reliable in the primary grades. Young children are inexperienced in taking tests. They have difficulty following directions and determining correct responses. Some schools give practice tests in kindergarten through second grade. Other schools wait until the third grade before giving standardized tests.

What are standardized tests? They are tests that are considered objective because they are administered in the same manner, with the same directions, to children at the same grade level all across the country. They measure student performance in norms, percentiles, and stanines that allow children to be compared to other children, and schools to be compared with other schools. The results of standardized tests can be, and are, used in a number of different ways. Some of the most common uses are to determine the strengths and weaknesses of the educational program; to inform teachers and parents about the academic growth of individual students; and to identify those children who may have learning problems or who score exceptionally high and need a more challenging school experience. Standardized tests often serve as criteria for pull-out programs for exceptional children who need additional support at either end of the learning continuum.

If your child will be given a standardized test this year, prepare her by briefly discussing the purpose of the test in a low-key manner— "to help your teacher decide what to teach next," or "to help your teacher teach you well"— and by making sure that your child has plenty of sleep and a good breakfast on the day of the test. It's in your child's best interest not to put too much emotional weight on the test or the test results. If you are anxious, you will likely convey that anxiety to your child, and any undue tension will hinder rather than help her performance.

Most schools that use standardized testing send the results home. When you receive the results, read the instruction book carefully to learn how to interpret them. If you have any questions regarding what the different numbers mean, contact the school principal and request an explanation. Don't be embarrassed or intimidated. Educators often get a crash course in deciphering the code each year. If your school doesn't send the results home, and you would like to know how your child fared, call the principal as well. If the test booklet becomes part of your child's school records, you are permitted by law to view it.

You may feel that the test results accurately reflect what you know about your child. If you feel, however, that there is a discrepancy between how your child performs in the classroom and how she performed on the test, by all means speak with your child's teacher. Ask whether the results of the test are consistent with your child's performance. Keep in mind that many circumstances can affect test results. If your child didn't feel well, was unable to concentrate, or incorrectly interpreted the directions, the results will not be valid. If the teacher agrees that the test results are grossly inconsistent with your child's performance, and if the test will play a part in your child's education— for instance, in determining which reading or math group she'll be placed in— you may request that she take the test again. Testing companies can and will provide alternative tests.

Standardized tests can be used positively to inform schools, teachers, and parents. They can also be overused. Sometimes this limited—and, yes, flawed— form of measurement is used to determine whether a child should be promoted or retained, whether a child does or does not qualify for special services, whether a teacher is successful, and whether or not a school system is worthy of government funds or special grants. But a standardized test should never be the sole consideration in making important educational decisions—particularly those that affect individual children. Whenever there are educational decisions to be made, observational and assessment data from the child's teacher, parents, and, in some cases, specialists should be included in the decision-making process.

Observing Your Child in the Classroom

Undoubtedly the best way to collect information about your child's school experience is to observe the class in action. You may want to observe for a crucial hour, a morning, or a full day. With advance notice, most schools welcome parent observers. Send a note to your child's teacher (*not* the principal) first. Explain that you are working with your child at home and would like to learn more about the curriculum and her teaching methods. By watching, you'll be able to help your child in a more consistent manner. Don't be shy about offering to help as well as observe—the more direct contact you have, the better. Keep in mind that not every day is necessarily a good time to observe (the children may be at gym or participating in a special event), and most teachers would prefer that you not come in September when classroom routines and rules are just being established. Be aware, as well, that your child may not behave the same way while you are observing as he would if you were not present.

If you have time, volunteer to help out in your child's classroom on a regular basis. Being a regular visitor will allow you, your child's teacher, and your child to relax into more consistent, normal behavior. Take your cues from the teacher, and try not to offer suggestions too often. Let the teacher know how much you enjoy being in the classroom. If a concern arises, schedule a conference with the teacher just as you would if you and she were not working side by side.

Even if you can't come in to school once a week, offer to help out with a special project or go along on a field trip. As you work with your child's classmates, you will discover a great deal about how children learn at this grade level and more about the academic goals. Your child will see firsthand how much you value education and will feel proud of your participation. These small acts will go a long way in helping your child succeed in school.

Appendixes

The Alphabet Connection Word Family List

....

ab:	cab, dab, gab, jab, lab, nab, tab, grab
ad:	bad, cad, dad, fad, lad, mad, pad, sad, glad
ag:	bag, gag, lag, nag, rag, sag, tag, brag, wag, crag, drag, flag, snag
am:	am, dam, ham, jam, Pam, ram, Sam, clam, sham, slam, tram, scram
an:	an, ban, can, Dan, fan, man, Nan, pan, ran, tan, van, bran, plan
ap:	cap, gap, lap, map, nap, rap, sap, tap, chap, clap, slap, snap, trap
ar:	bar, car, far, jar, tar
at:	at, bat, cat, fat, hat, mat, pat, rat, sat, vat, drat, flat, slat, that
ay:	bay, day, hay, jay, lay, May, pay, ray, say, way, clay, gray, play
ed:	bed, fed, led, red, Ted, wed, bled, fled, shed, sled
eg:	beg, keg, leg, peg
en:	Ben, den, hen, men, pen, ten, glen, then, when
et:	bet, get, jet, let, met, net, pet, set, vet, wet
id:	bid, did, hid, kid, lid, rid, skid, slid
ig:	big, dig, fig, jig, pig, rig, wig
in:	in, bin, din, fin, kin, pin, sin, tin, win, chin, grin, shin, skin, spin, thin, twin
ip:	dip, hip, lip, rip, sip, tip
it:	it, bit, fit, hit, kit, lit, pit, sit, wit, flit, knit, quit, slit, spit
ob:	Bob, cob, job, lob, mob, rob, sob, blob, slob, snob
op:	bop, cop, hop, mop, pop, top

ot: cot, dot, got, hot, jot, lot, not, pot, rot, tot, blot, clot, knot, plot, shot, slot, spot, trot

ub: cub, hub, rub, sub, tub

ud: bud, cud, dud, mud, spud, thud

ug: bug, dug, hug, jug, rug, tug

um: bum, gum, hum, rum, sum

un: bun, fun, gun, nun, run, sun, shun, spun, stun

up: up, cup, pup, sup

ut: but, cut, gut, hut, jut, nut, rut

ack: back, hack, jack, lack, pack, sack, black, quack, stack, smack, snack, track, shack

age: cage, page, sage, rage, wage, stage

aid: braid, maid, paid, raid

ake: bake, cake, fake, lake, make, rake, sake, take, wake, stake, brake, flake, snake, quake, shake

and: and, band, hand, land, bland, brand, grand, stand

eat: eat, beat, feat, heat, meat, neat, peat, seat, bleat, cheat, pleat, treat, wheat

eed: deed, feed, need, seed, weed, bleed, greed, speed

eek: meek, peek, seek, creek, cheek, sleek

eel: feel, heel, peel, steel, wheel

eep: beep, deep, jeep, keep, peep, seep, weep, creep, sleep, sweep, sheep

eet: beet, feet, meet, greet, sheet, tweet

ent: bent, dent, lent, rent, sent, tent, vent, went, spent

ile: file, mile, pile, tile, while

ine: dine, fine, line, mine, nine, pine, vine, wine, shine, spine, twine, whine

ing: ding, king, ring, sing, wing, bring, cling, fling, sting, swing

ink: link, mink, pink, sink, wink, blink, brink, clink, drink, stink, think

int: hint, lint, mint, tint, flint, stint

oil: oil, boil, coil, foil, soil, broil, spoil

oke: Coke, joke, poke, woke, broke, choke, smoke, spoke

old: old, bold, cold, fold, gold, hold, mold, sold, told, scold

ook: book, cook, hook, look, nook, took, brook, crook, shook

ool: cool, pool, tool, spool, stool

ore: ore, bore, core, more, sore, tore, chore, shore, store

orn: born, corn, horn, morn, worn, sworn

unk: bunk, dunk, hunk, junk, sunk, chunk, clunk, drunk, skunk, spunk, stunk, trunk

High-Frequency Bookwords

Final core 227-word list based on 400 storybooks for beginning readers

the	good	think	next	and	this	new
only	a	don't	know	am	I	little
help	began	to	if	grand	head	said
just	boy	keep	you	baby	take	teacher
he	way	eat	sure	it	there	body
says	in	every	school	ride	was	went
house	pet	she	father	morning	hurry	for
had	yes	hand	that	see	after	hard
is	dog	never	push	his	home	or
our	but	down	self	their	they	got
try	watch	my	would	has	because	of
time	always	door	on	love	over	us
me	walk	again	should	all	came	side
room	be	were	thank	pull	go	ask
why	great	can	back	who	gave	with
now	saw	does	one	friend	mom	car
her	cry	kid	ball	what	oh	give
sat	we	Mr.	around	stay	him	bed
by	each	no	an	Mrs.	ever	so

very	off	until	out	where	sister	shout
up	play	find	mama	are	let	fun
use	will	long	more	turn	look	here
while	thought	some	how	tell	papa	day
make	sleep	lot	at	big	made	blue
have	from	first	bath	your	put	say
mean	mother	read	took	sit	come	them
dad	together	not	as	found	best	like
Miss	lady	brother	then	any	soon	feel
get	right	ran	floor	when	nice	dear
wait	thing	other	man	tomorrow	do	well
better	surprise	too	old	through	shop	want
night	stop	run	did	may	still	own
could	about	fast				

From Maryann Eeds, "Bookwords: Using a Beginning Word List of High Frequency Words from Children's Literature K–3," *The Reading Teacher* 38(4), 418–23. Copyright © 1985 by the International Reading Association. All rights reserved.

Index

Activity Pages

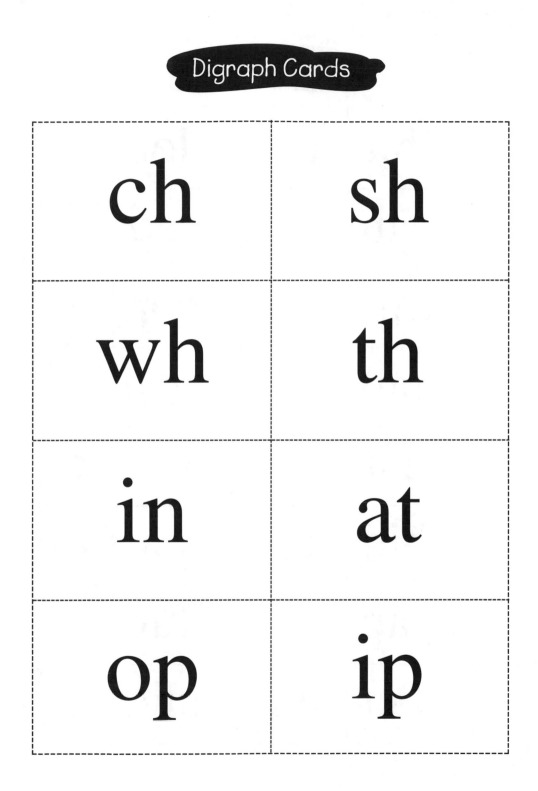

ch	sh
wh	th
in	at
op	ip

Silent "e" Cards

bit	e	glob	e
can	e	mad	e
strip	e	hop	e
tap	e	rip	e
hat	e	not	e
hid	e	pal	e
scrap	e	tub	e
Pet	e	slid	e

Alphabet Chart

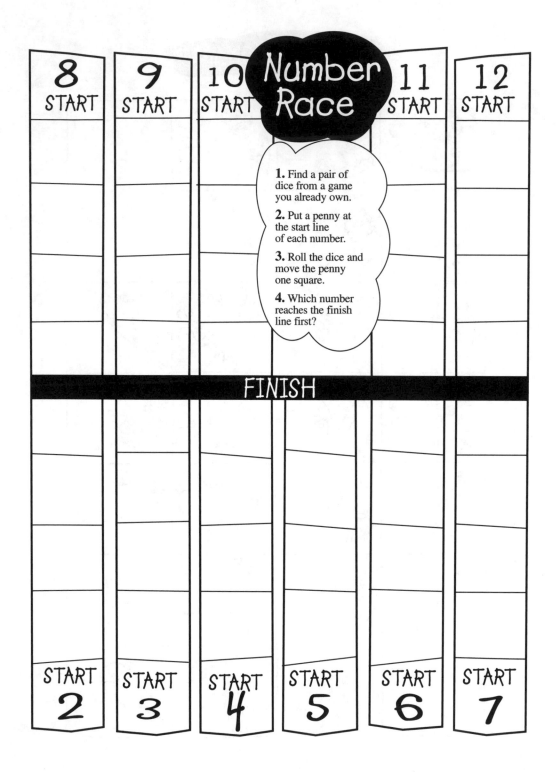

Number Race

8 START
9 START
10 START
11 START
12 START

1. Find a pair of dice from a game you already own.

2. Put a penny at the start line of each number.

3. Roll the dice and move the penny one square.

4. Which number reaches the finish line first?

FINISH

START 2
START 3
START 4
START 5
START 6
START 7

0-99 Grid

0	1	2	3	4	5	6	7	8	9
10	11	12	13	14	15	16	17	18	19
20	21	22	23	24	25	26	27	28	29
30	31	32	33	34	35	36	37	38	39
40	41	42	43	44	45	46	47	48	49
50	51	52	53	54	55	56	57	58	59
60	61	62	63	64	65	66	67	68	69
70	71	72	73	74	75	76	77	78	79
80	81	82	83	84	85	86	87	88	89
90	91	92	93	94	95	96	97	98	99

Number Train

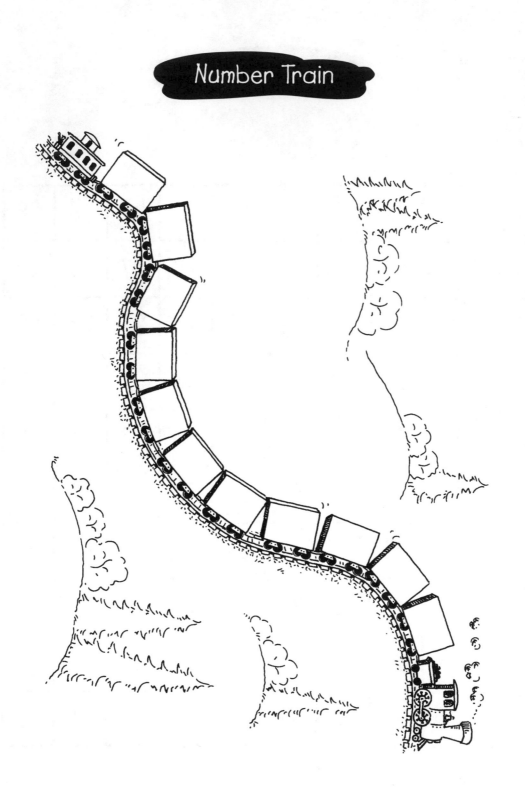